WINGS O
THE VAL

A Bird Watcher's Wales Diary

JOHN GREEN

First published in Britain 2000 by Artery Publications, 11 Dorset Road, London W5 4HU
Copyright © John Green 2000
Illustrations by John Green
Designed by Artloud. Tel: (0) 207 686 6111
Printed by Cambrian Printers, Llanbadarn Road, Aberystwyth SY23 3TN. Tel: 01970 627111
A CIP catalogue record for this book is available from the British Library
ISBN 09513909 5 3

WINGS OVER THE VALLEY

A Bird Watcher's Wales Diary

I've travelled the world,
seen sights and met fascinating people,
but only when I returned home
did I become aware
of the beauty
on my own doorstep

Rabindranath Tagore

Other books by the author:

In Search of Birds in Mid-Wales (together with Brian O'Shea)
In Search of Birds in the Scottish Highlands (together with Brian O'Shea)
Birds in and around Ealing
Taking the Pulse - memoirs of a TV correspondent
In Love and Anger (poetry)

This diary would not have been written without the encouragement and companionship on many a bird-watching outing of my friend Brian O'Shea, who introduced me to this fascinating area of Wales. Thanks are due also to Brunhild, Galina and Siski for reading the first drafts and making constructive criticisms.

I dedicate it, though, to my mother, Marguerite Morgan, without whose selfless support and inspiration I would probably never have discovered my love of birds, the countryside and of language.

CONTENTS

Buzzard pair

INTRODUCTION

I walk up the lane, through a narrow gap between a palisade of slender oaks and larches, to face a fortification of hills. In the cleavage between them three cottages are lodged, like pebbles. High above them, a small dark cross, framed by a tower of luminous white cloud, catches my eye as it rises over the crest. It floats towards me and the sun sets it alight, turning it into a bird with fiery plumage. Its forked tail rudders it gently around and the wind wafts it slowly up the valley, where the mountains swallow it once more. I feel drawn to follow, caught in its spell. At this moment I know I'll settle here.

The buzzards and kites belong to these valleys as gulls do to the coast. They define the contours and give significance to the freedom of space. Their flight sketches in the missing dimensions and lends the hills their special aura, they are the true spirits of the valleys.

It is, though, the kite more than any other bird which has drawn me here. In Wales one of several names given to the kite is 'boda gwennol' or swallow harrier and this seems to me a particularly apt description. Like the buzzard, it can be seen hugging the ridges of the hills or spiraling on the thermals, often together with buzzards. However, unlike the buzzard, which is lumbering and not at all nimble, the kite moves in the air like a swallow, turning, tacking, swooping and soaring with sublime agility. It is a slim bird and, seen from the side, it seems to have no body at all, but to be all wings and tail. It has a massive wing-span of nearly two metres and, although considerably smaller than Britain's two indigenous eagles, is only marginally so than the osprey. When flapping leisurely over the hills its wing beats seem laboured and it is difficult to imagine that this slow-moving bird could be an agile aeronaut, but when it is dodging crows or robbing them of food morsels its efficient manoeuvrability becomes abundantly clear. Its large wing and tail area give it excellent uplift and it can remain in the air for hours with scarcely a wing beat. It is not surprising that paper and cloth kites were named after the bird.

Although kites and buzzards appear to make use of similar food sources, conflict between the two species is rare. I've never seen them attacking each other or squabbling, but, on the contrary, observe them often circling amicably together.

THE DIARY

Sifting through my diaries and writing them up in book form has been like the work of a photographer developing his prints in the darkroom. Half-eclipsed events and fragments of memory attain a new clarity and a connectedness as the images crystalise on the page.

This diary is a compression of several years' observations in and around a typical valley in mid-Wales, situated close to the Cardigan Bay coast. Everything mentioned is based on first-hand experience at the time of year given. It reflects faithfully my own observations throughout the year, but includes some made by my close companion who introduced me to many of the area's secrets and was with me on many of the outings. I have, though, been selective, weeding out entries of the many days when very little of interest was seen or heard, or when the weather was too atrocious for man or beast to venture abroad.

Sequences of landscape descriptions can be tedious; it is what happens in and to a landscape that lends it interest. Here I've used the birds as the key to open up the landscapes which are their home and provide their sustenance.

Everything I describe could have been seen or heard easily by anyone else, but hardly in its entirety in any single year. My aim is to capture the inexorable flow and rhythm of the seasons as they impinge on this mid-Wales valley. I've tried to freeze this process and to communicate the exhilaration, the enjoyment and spiritual fulfillment this fragile world still offers the sensitive observer.

Although life has not remained untouched by the changes of recent decades, the impact of technology, the inuredness of mercenary attitudes and communal alienation has not penetrated here so profoundly as elsewhere. The hedges may now be flayed by machinery, the shepherds and farm labourers almost an extinct breed, the rural omnibus given way to the car, but in many ways life has not drastically changed. Precisely because it is one of the few places in Britain unconnected by motorways or fast rail links, it has developed no real industrial infrastructure or mass tourism. The dour villages of grey stone and the expanses of wild moor are not attractive to most town-dwellers and the poor, thin soil does not offer the promise of lucrative returns to big farmers. Hill sheep farming is virtually the only feasible livelihood.

Given that it is the kite more than any other creature that epitomises these valleys, the opportunity afforded for watching other attractive birds of prey is an added bonus of living here.

Mid-Wales has probably the highest density of raptors of anywhere in the British Isles and boasts a large number of breeding species: Buzzards, kites, peregrines, kestrels, sparrowhawks, goshawks, merlins and hen harriers as well as tawny, long-eared and barn owls.

In this diary I have used the breeding cycles and movements of the birds of prey as a sort of barometer and guide. As they are usually the most visible of the birds and remain in or around the valley all year round, they are ideal subjects to follow.

THE VALLEY

Imagine two enormous dinosaurs dying alongside each other millennia ago. In the intervening years their backs have been scoured by the winds and greened by invading plant life. In the narrow gap between their adjacent bodies a small, fast-flowing rivulet has been formed by the copious rainfall running down their sides and trees have sprouted along its route. That describes the valley where I live. The surrounding mountains wear the frowns, wrinkles and scars of immeasurable time. From any of the higher peaks the whole area resembles a dinosaur graveyard, with bare, rounded humps piled up to the horizons.

It was in secluded valleys just like this where four or five red kite pairs escaped extinction during the earlier part of this century. Through the valiant efforts of a small dedicated band of conservationists, aided by the natural barriers of mountains and low population, the birds miraculously survived. The kite has thus become a symbol of resilience and of the will to survive. It is an extraordinary example of the rugged beauty of Wales.

On the valley's south-eastern side are hedged fields leading up to the bracken and gorse-covered slopes and the bare summit, while its north-western side is densely wooded with larch, spruce and oak. At its head it opens out onto the bleakness of the high moor. The sharp contour line of the bare hills descends to meet the valley and contnues in a soft serpentine of rowans which traces the stream's course. A steep, winding lane provides access from a lower, broader valley, where the stream forms a confluence with a larger river which carries the meandering swollen waters to the sea. From the valley floor at 50 metres, the surrounding hills rise to almost 350 metres.

The small cottage which is my home, snuggles into the northern face of one hill and looks out over the valley, bisected by its small stream that has carved steep banks where the earth is soft and gravelly. If there were no hills on the horizon I would see the sea six miles away. Sometimes, when the light blurs those hills into pastel blues and the heat causes the light to vibrate, I imagine I am watching the sea.

A hazel-fringed flinty cart track leads up from the lane to the cottage. On the uphill side of the path is a small hanging oak wood, light and airy, with good ground vegetation. On the lower side is a field where cows or sheep are brought in spring or late summer to be fattened up on the rich pasture. A large, ivy-entwined ash tree with spreading arms like a protective mother stands in front of the cottage, and on the far side, like sentries, a pair of tall fir trees.

This ash tree has a small ecosystem of its own. On one occasion in late spring, while sitting close to the tree, I saw within a short while several goldfinches settle in it, a male redstart, a male pied flycatcher, great and coal tits searching for grubs, a great spotted woodpecker, a crow, blackbird, a pair of chaffinches, a singing garden and willow warbler, as well as a curious grey squirrel!

On the small terrace adjoining the cottage, thick slices of spruce trunks, their orange heartwood wrapped in chocolate-brown bark, lie stacked, like giant pieces of confectionery. This is fuel for the winter fire. In Autumn and Winter wrens and tits rummage through it in search of sheltering insects and larvae. In spring, pied flycatchers and blue tits alternate in their use of the nest box on the wall.

The sky in Wales is a constant source of drama and change. I can often sit for hours on the terrace, watching the sky endlessly mutating into fascinating shapes and colours: blue skies filling with ballooning clouds which either race through the heavens like mad sheep or sit sedately on the hills like enormous Restoration perriwigs; cobalt blues melting into leaden greys and, in the evenings, into blood-drenched sunsets before night ousts the light from the valley. At times the light is of such clarity that it appears to be unmediated by the atmosphere. If it's a cloudless night and the air is crisp and clear, the constellations glisten with stabbing sharpness, like lights behind a moth-eaten, velvet gown. Here they are undimmed by the scatter-glow of street lights or other urban luminosity. It is an astronomer's dream. And the full moon, like a giant Stilton, rolls in silence over the slumbering hills or, waning, shyly reveals only a sliver of crescent light.

In summer there is an atmosphere of sluggish peace, of richness and fulfillment. Nature has achieved its goal - eggs have hatched and fledglings flown, stigmas have been pollinated and fruits begun to ripen, butterflies and moths flutter out their last few days or weeks. The cows in the field below the cottage lounge lethargically, grinding the cud mechanically with their jaws. The sheep work their way slowly through the ffridd* on the hillsides, nibbling without pause to renew their coats for the coming autumn. Only the subdued rustle of leaves, the chuntering of the stream and distant ruminant munching can be heard above the quietude.

The air is heavy with the ambrosial scents of mountain ash and may blossom and the valley lies with open arms, its recumbent hills clad voluptuously in soft greenery, as if awaiting a lover.

The small crisp-green valley fields are delineated by irregular rows of mature oak, ash and alder; the hill tops are fringed by dark stands of spruce and fir. Dry stone walls, falling increasingly into disrepair, mark the old boundaries of the hill farms. Now their only function is to provide nesting holes for wheatears, redstarts and tits or sheltering shade for the sheep. Their stones are etched and tattooed with patterns of yellow and grey lichens. At the foot of the valley there used to be a Roman fort. Only a pale reminder is there now, in the shadowed undulations beneath the grass, where its walls once stood.

The ruins of the old lead mines in the upper valley scar the landscape, surrounded as they are by slag heaps of grey, poisonous stone - silent memorials to a vibrant industrial past. In the last century the mines supported a not insignificant workforce and the miners' stone dwellings formed huddled communities in the valleys. With the decline in the need for lead and the introduction of more efficient mining techniques

---

*(Fridd is a Welsh term which describes that typical area of mountain slope between the valley pastures below and the rough moorland or crags above. It is characterised by its rough mixture of vegetation - bracken, hawthorn, heather and bilberry)

elsewhere, the mines fell into desuetude. A colony of jackdaws now occupies the holes and crevices in the remaining walls, alongside polypodium ferns which have established a precarious foothold in the crumbling mortar. On the slag heaps two pairs of wheatears regularly breed and on the stream that flows alongside, a pair of pied wagtails proclaim riparian ownership.

The soil in this part of the country is poor - barely a skin covering the hard Silurian rock that lies beneath. Where winds and rain have worn away the topsoil, jagged bones of rock protrude through the torn skin, providing the few modest cliffs for peregrines and ravens. Where the rock has crumbled to form screes, wheatears and even the rare ring ouzel make their homes. It is not surprising that the area remained relatively undeveloped, supporting only a few poor hill farmers. Wales didn't have the landed gentry of Scotland and the heather moors were not so widespread. Game was scarce (although even scarcer today) and there are as yet virtually no deer, so gamekeeping was and is a rare occupation. This goes some way in explaining a number of significant differences between the fauna of the two countries. The hill moors in mid-Wales are desolate and bare: wide expanses of tough mat grass, rush and moss, with patches of heather and bilberry. The cliffs at their margins are like elephant skin - hard, grey and deeply creviced.

The rawness is an expression of that strength and dignity that only comes from struggle - the scars, frowns and wrinkles are not just the outer signs of ageing, but the record of a momentous struggle against the elements and against man. And the birds that today still inhabit the nooks and crevices in this landscape also reflect and represent that long war of attrition that is continuing today.

This area has its own micro-climate where I can be basking in the sun one minute while only a mile or so higher up the valley it will be raining or snowing. If the valley is enveloped in cloud however, the coast may have brilliant sunshine. In winter we are lucky if a light dusting of snow falls. The prevailing Gulf Stream keeps the weather mild, even at the height of winter. When the strong South-westerlies are funnelled up the valley, though, it can bend the trees to their tensile limits and set the rafters of the cottage creaking. Then I feel as if I am living in the slipstream of a giant jet. Sometimes the clouds descend to form a low ceiling, pressing down on you or they may build up into gigantic walls, like a Tower of Babel, being erected on the mountains.

Westerly winds often bring sea mists curling up the valley to shroud the woods and hills till they are almost completely obliterated, leaving the valley marooned in a no-man's-land of eerie silence. On such days I can smell sea salt in the air.

The seasons are markedly different from each other and unlike in a large city, where seasonal change is largely masked by concrete and brick, here you are constantly reminded of the annual cycle: skeletal trees bursting into greenery and woods becoming impenetrable, lane-side verges donning raucous colour and mushrooms sprouting from nowhere and then green hills turning rusty again as autumn nudges aside the late summer.

The Forestry Commission has created great swathes of forest, over the decades since the last war, where once were only bare hills. This has not only radically altered the landscape visually, but it has also brought with it enormous changes to the wildlife of the area. Goshawks, crossbills and siskins, as well as hares, once absent or very scarce have benefited significantly. Over 130 species of bird breed in the area regularly, even if some do so only as single pairs or in small numbers. There are an additional 30 or more species which visit each year as non-breeding migrants, and then there are rarities like white-tailed sea eagle or great grey shrike which show up on occasion.

Sheep farmers, aided by mechanisation and seduced by subsidies, are clearing the last remnants of heather and wetland, so that ever more sheep can be reared. But despite all this, the area still remains one of the wilder and relatively unspoiled parts of the British isles. It can't stay this way. So-called progress is unstoppable, as is population pressure. Its relative ease of access, together with increased leisure time is also having an impact. Already on Bank Holidays motocross teams or rally drivers descend here to shatter the calm with their souped-up vehicles, and holiday caravans clog the main access roads.

It gives me cause to wonder whether future generations will be able to watch kites sailing over ancient oak woods, dippers diving into sparkling unsullied streams or hear the music of the wind, the gurgle of a brook without the irritating background hum of vehicles, canned music or drone of planes. Sometimes I am filled with doubt. I would like to hope they will, but this hope is tempered by a deep scepticism about whether my fellow human beings see the dangers, are prepared to confront them and work out solutions. It is, after all, we humans who create policies, economies and environmental problems and it is only we who can change them. There is no such thing as fate, we alone, in our inter-relationships, manufacture our own lives and futures - and a future without the freedom to roam nature's wildernesses will, in my opinion, hardly be worth striving for. I suppose it is these doubts which have given impetus to my decision to write this diary. It is an attempt to capture and preserve for posterity an imprint, even if only a shadowy one, of life in these valleys before memories become silted-up by irrevocable change.

I often used to drive to the area before I eventually settled, and each time I felt as if I were fleeing a storm-driven tidal wave to enter a calm haven. The heavy drone of traffic and roads choked with speeding metal slowly gave way to country lanes with only the occasional car and then to mountain roads where sheep were virtually the only traffic. I'm appalled at the destruction motor traffic causes today, even where it is less dense. Roads have become the modern killing fields, littered with the corpses of badgers, foxes, hedgehogs, pheasants and song birds. Drivers career along at maximum speed, uncaring of the world around them, killing with brutalised indifference. I am relieved that, for me, these journeys are no longer necessary.

BEING A SLEUTH

Urban noise and hectic movement are reduced to a faded nightmare in the valley. Nature here appears to dictate the pace and draws you imperceptibly into its rhythm. Although you are an interloper, a spy, you are nevertheless tolerated and life takes its course around you, paying little notice to your presence.

Your aim is to merge as best you can into the background, become like a tree or rock, an accepted part of the natural environment, so that you can watch animal behaviour unobserved or at least ignored, to discover where territories are being established, where nest-building is taking place, or where pairs are displaying and posturing. You become a detective, following clues and leads, observing suspects, noting, evaluating and interpreting behaviour, establishing where events are taking place. There is the constant expectation of something appearing over the brows of the hills, something dramatic happening just out of view. The main difference between a nature sleuth and the work of a real life criminologist is that here there are no 'criminals' to be brought to court. There may be murders or theft, but these aren't illegal, they are part of the natural order and serve the flow and flux of this fragile ecosystem.

Birds, particularly when they are far away, in silhouette or only glimpsed as a smudge of plumage, are not always easy to recognise. The guide books show you them in full colour close-up, perfectly lit and static on the page. These illustrations often bear little resemblance to what you actually see. Identifying birds is not really about eye-stripes, wing bars or leg colour, as important as these can be on occasion, but more about a bird's personality. Each species has its own special intangible character or 'aura' and even without the vital clues of colour or size you can learn to recognise them. Although I can still embarrassingly - and this may surprise or shock the uninitiated - confuse a skylark with a merlin or a raven with a buzzard, despite the enormous size and colour differences between them. Such confusions are usually only momentary ones, but still happen. In the wide open spaces, often with no trees or objects against which to estimate size, it can be very difficult.

It isn't just a matter of the bird itself, however. Landscape and terrain are also vital clues to identification. Observing the valley and nearby coastal birds over many years, I've become intimately acquainted with their territories and am able to judge exactly what sort of vegetation they require or prefer. I could take you to many places and, at a specific time of the year, guarantee that you would see a particular species. Then, on the other hand, there are numerous places I would normally consider ideal for certain species, yet I never encounter them there. Why, I don't know. For instance, most upland lakes and pools in the area lack birds altogether, yet one, apparently no different from the others may hold one or several species. This is often connected with water acidity, but that alone cannot account for the discrepancies. Birds common in more Eastern parts of Britain, like coots, moorhens or yellow wagtails, are rarities here, often only one or two pairs. Other birds common in these oak woods, like pied flycatchers, are not at all common in similar oak woods in England. It is these apparent inconsistencies and surprises that make bird watching so tantalising and interesting.

SPRING

Little ringed plovers

SPRING

In early spring the countryside simulates lifelessness, but as winter recedes, you can sense beneath the dead leaf scrolls and bare branches an impatient stirring. There is a vibrancy in the air and a throbbing beneath the fragile skin. Resident birds are singing and hopping about in the trees like fleas, energised by their concupiscense. Beneath the bud scales and the surface of the soil new life is surging upward. Spring emerges from winter like a young bird from its egg - expected, but with surprising abruptness. Before you have really become aware of a change, it bursts, thin veined from its prison integuments. An infectious fecundity takes hold. The hawthorn is among the first to break into leaf, feathering the spiky hedges with soft greenery, then honeysuckle and elder; bluebell spears pierce the forest floor and hedge banks are transformed into flower gardens. These blossoms, though, are more than just a beautiful backdrop. They provide vital food for the insects which in turn give sustenance to our summer migrants.

Spring begins in the lower, shallower valleys first, where the probing fingers of the sun reach with the lengthening of the days. Only much later does it gain the courage to embrace the moors and mountain tops, where late frosts and unseasonable snowstorms persist.

11 MARCH

The hills are wrapped in a light mist. The bracken, woods and grass merge into a flat panorama of soft, intermingling aquatints. The plaintive bleating of new born lambs and the growing volume and intensity of bird song fill the air. As the morning progresses, the mist slowly dissipates even from the upper valley.

I take the small footpath that leads to a rusty iron gate, kept closed by a ring of twisted wire. It continues alongside the brook that flows down through the alder carr, where I have put up some nest boxes for the expected pied flycatchers, then it follows a tall hazel hedge through a small field towards the old plantation. This field is usually left unmown and the grass grows long and thick. In late summer it is a profusion of meadow flowers, but at this time of year they are still dormant.

From the edge of the plantation narrow tracks have been trampled in the grass, leading down towards the stream - they are made by badgers and foxes coming from the wood at night to drink.

From the field, the path hugs the tall larches at the edge of the plantation and then rises more steeply, becoming very slippery in damp weather. On the far side of the stream, on the north-western hillside, small hawthorns and gorse scrub have found a hold on the thin soil. Where the plantation comes to an end, the track leads up through heather and bracken to the summit, crowned by a small copse of stately and ancient beech trees. Just beyond the summit, framed by the silver-grey trunks of the beeches and cradled by the surrounding hills is a small lake. Beyond it is a second lake at the head of the adjoining valley, and at one end a large derelict farm house commands the view that no one now enjoys from its dusty windows. Rusting old tractors and binders occupy the silent yard and barns.

From the beech copse, looking towards the West I can see the whole length of the valley to the sea, and behind me, to the East the wild expanse of the upland moors. Although it is mild in the valleys, it is still very cold on those moors where a light drizzle is falling as snow, transforming the usually dark hills into mounds of china clay.

A kite is circling above the beech copse as I approach, and a sentinel buzzard reluctantly takes off from its fence post with laboured wing beats. It joins two others high in the sky and all three then proceed to play dive, retracting their wings, plummeting down and then braking and veering off before impact. They do this for several minutes before spiraling off to the west. I can hear no human voices up here. I feel strangely vulnerable, cut off from the comforting sounds of human habitations. I am alone with the kites, the trees and the ever inconstant sky.

The resident pair of ravens becomes aware of my presence and they begin croaking their annoyance. They have an ancient nest site in an old fir, hidden in the depth of the wood which blankets the steep hillside down to the road. This site must have been used for many years, as the nest is almost two meters high - an enormous tower of sticks. I haven't visited it yet this year, but judging by the anxious behaviour of the adults, it probably contains eggs or even young by now.

On the first lake, shimmering in the clear light, a group of 15 pochards is diving in the deeper water, a pair of mallard slumber in the reeds fringing the shore and a heron stands stiffly in the willow scrub, scrutinising the still water with eyes like jewels mounted on its dagger beak.

As I wander through the crackling beech leaves down to the

Heron fishing

lakeside, a peregrine lurches from a small pine growing out of the rock and peels off over the lake. It is a sure sign that the birds of prey are beginning to return to their hilly domains, because it's the first one I've seen up here since last autumn. Slowly I begin to feel at home. These are the birds I know. I'm accustomed to their shapes, their voices and behavioural patterns. To me they're friends, even though to them I'm merely a minor irritant, interrupting their routines.

Close by I pass a sheep carcass on the hill. I don't know how many days or weeks it has lain here, because putrefaction is a slow process in these cold, clean hills. Its eyes are hollow button holes in its fleecy head and clots of wool lie scattered in a circle around the corpse, like a halo. Its taut amber skin is bared to the wind which plays on the comb of its exposed ribs, picked clean by the kites, buzzards and ravens. Lying there, open to the elements, it attains a certain morbid aesthetic dignity. Death in these hills is an essential factor of life's dialectic. Without it none of the magnificent birds of prey could survive. I can't help feeling that, for this sheep, death in its own domain is preferable to being a victim of mass execution in an abattoir, reeking of panic.

The second lake is empty save for a rusty-headed female merganser, which hopefully may consider nesting. The surrounding hills are mirrored in the water's unruffled surface until a trout noses the meniscus and corrugates the inverted sky. The merganser watches anxiously as I approach and swims farther out towards the middle, but doesn't fly. I take the path away from the lake and begin my descent home, leaving the merganser in peace.

I'm on the lookout for a second kite pair. I know there is one close by, but the birds can hide amazingly easily in a fold of the hills or in one of the small woods that clothe the slopes. Like a begging bowl, the sky remains empty despite my urgent wish to have it filled.

My descent home takes me past the copse again and a pair of jays clatter out of an ancient beech, their rasping voices shattering the tranquillity, scolding me back down the hill. The small cross of a kite appears in the sky about a quarter of a mile away to my left, over the hill. It glides parallel with me, watching to ensure I am leaving the territory. As I turn the bend in the lane, it rises and disappears over the ridge, satisfied I'm no longer a danger.

As the day drains slowly into the late afternoon, the woods and hedges fall silent as their denizens await the respite of night. Dusk lays a caressing hand of soft pink on the breast of the recumbent mountain. The cottage becomes a womb and my small log fire exudes a foetal warmth. Outside the velvet sensuality of night swirls in pregnant anticipation of a new day.

13 MARCH

The sun plays hide and seek behind the fast moving clouds. Along the stream, small flocks of siskins and redpolls are flitting through the alder crowns, but soon they will be splitting up into pairs to begin nest building. Nuthatches are calling to each other, warbling their short melodic song from two tall ashes growing by the stream among the alder carr.

I've just finished breakfast, and am staring absent-mindedly out of the window, when I spot two kites, which look like a pair, twirling and interweaving over the beech copse on the hill at the head of the valley. They dive playfully at each other and then sheer away. They perform these games for almost a quarter of an hour before drifting off over the lake to the North-west. I'm thrilled and decide to give them names, feeling sure I will be seeing much more of them in the coming months: Snowyhead for the male and Rusty for the female. This personalises them, gives them a status above being mere 'kites' and links them firmly to the valley!

Most mornings now, I am greeted by one of the kites or the pair over the cottage, usually circling leisurely, checking the terrain, before drifting off to the upper valley or over the ridge to an adjoining one. I don't attempt to follow them as they are very sensitive to disturbances at this time of the year when establishing or re-establishing nesting territories and need peace and quiet, to feel secure enough to begin building. The local buzzard pair is mewing from the woods and above the north-west ridge a skylark's song tumbles out of the sky.

14 MARCH

Over the sea the sky looks brighter and the cloud thinner than over the hills where it is still dark and threatening. A walk along the coast makes good sense today, although even here there is unlikely to be much life. Like the tourists, most birds will be reluctant to chance the still unpredictable weather and will await warmer days. The wind coming off the sea is still bitingly cold and a weak sun is trying desperately to break through the layers of low-lying cloud. The slopes of the hills that form a backdrop to the beach are splattered with clumps of bright yellow gorse like dollops of butter between the hawthorns.

A few gulls flutter aimlessly just off the beach, others shelter in the lee of the groynes. Oystercatchers and curlews forage in small groups at the tide's edge. It is still too early and too cold for them to be tempted away to their nesting areas. I scan the waters and locate some small, tight groups of black ducks, which appear and disappear among the waves. Suddenly something large breaks surface close to these over-wintering scoters: three pelagic dolphins leap through the air and dive again in perfect arcs, revealing their blunt snouts, dorsal fins and gleaming silvered backs.

29 MARCH

Today I am excited to hear my first chiffchaff of the year calling from the wood behind the cottage. He is a sure harbinger of spring. It is one of our first summer migrants to return, although in recent decades, possibly in connection with global warming, increasing numbers over winter in the milder parts of Britain and avoid the arduous oversea return journeys. Its song is an apt accompaniment to the flowering primroses, violets and sorrel, now necklacing the hedge banks.

Seeing familiar birds again in Spring after the long Winter shakes childhood memories from their ledges to tumble out in a cascade of cherished images. Whitethroats conjure up voluptuous country lanes, lace-edged with cow parsley and evanescent may-blossom; the tree pipit's parachute song is associated with slender birches shimmering on bracken covered heathland in the sharp Summer sun. Legs and arms scratched and bleeding from looking for nests in hawthorn thickets and clambering up hedge banks went unnoticed in the thrill of the search.

The hawthorn is now in full leaf and the birch buds are just breaking. In the larch plantation I catch a glimpse of two families of crossbills feeding high in the crowns - the pinky males, greenish females and more browny, streaked youngsters, probably not long flown from the nest. Crossbills, like ravens, are among our earliest breeding birds, ignoring late winter storms and the cold. They probably need to breed early so that the young can build up reserves from the cones, before they release their seeds in the late spring. Siskins are beginning to establish their territories and are performing aerial dances above the tall firs, calling excitedly as they do so.

In the neighbouring, 'Goosander valley' where a young couple are building a house in peasant Tudor style, two mistle thrushes are calling in limpid tremolos from the oak woods. These birds are popularly known as 'storm cocks' because of their predilection for singing in bad weather when most other birds are silent. Their strong fluting notes resounding from the top of a tall tree when the skies are dark and threatening is like a gauntlet heroically thrown down to the weather gods and is a real source of uplift for the spirit.

Pinned to the gatepost at the entrance to the farm, alongside the large wooden letter box, is a rough hand-written note asking the postman and visitors not to place letters in the box as a bluetit has made it its home there. As I stand looking at the house, a bluetit streaks past me and enters the slit in the box, as if to underline the truth of the note.

30 MARCH

Not far away, a few miles to the south of the cottage, is Wales's largest area of raised bog. In winter it is a favoured hunting ground for visiting raptors and on most days in summer kites and buzzards can be seen quartering its expanse. There are only two such bogs in mid-Wales, where the peat has been allowed to build up to considerable depths, thus lifting the bog's level. Others were destroyed by peat digging for fuel. This one lies at 150m above sea level in a flat valley, flanked by hills on its western edge and bisected by a small river. It is rich in specialised plants like sundew and St. John's wort, bog rosemary, as well as species of mosses. It also attracts a large variety of insects - butterflies like the fritillary, skipper, large heath and green hairstreak and a multitude of dragon, damsel and caddis flies. The bog comprises several square miles of rush, heath and heather, interrupted by small pools; there are large areas of rough pasture and wetland on which scattered clumps of willow flourish and the odd birch tree interrupts the flat expanse. A disused railway track traverses one side and its old hawthorn hedges provide refuge for finches, tits and pigeons. A walk

Curlew on nest

along this cutting provides excellent views over the expanse.

Its empty wasteland appearance is deceptive. Like an area of skin which only under the microscope reveals its menagerie of microbes, here too patient and close observation is essential to persuade it to reveal its secrets. As I scan the horizon, a female hen harrier emerges silently from behind a willow clump. She is clearly still reluctant to leave for the heather moors to begin breeding. With slow wing beats she quarters the rushes around the scrub, low over the ground, hoping to catch a vole sniffing the spring air, but she disappears again almost immediately into the depths of the scrub.

My curiosity is aroused by strong ripples, fanning out from the middle of a willow-fringed pool at the edge of the bog. I can't see any water birds and for a moment think it must be a large carp swimming at the surface. Looking through my binoculars I am thrilled to see it is an otter fishing. He dives and resurfaces with a flapping silver fish in his strong jaws, which he devours in seconds. I am able to watch it for almost a quarter of an hour swimming, circling, rolling and floating in the water. Its behaviour communicates the distinct impression that it is actually enjoying the freedom of this secluded pool. These animals are still very rare in Wales and I feel more than privileged to have witnessed this one. I hope it will be the beginning of a real come-back for these delightful mammals.

On leaving the bog, I disturb a crow nesting in a single, skinny birch tree alongside the old railway track. Below its nest is an owl box put there by the reserve's warden, and to my amazement a kestrel emerges and flies off low over the ground. Its nest in the box holds 5 eggs. I walk nimbly away to allow it to return.

Over an adjoining field, three curlews perform their slow undulating display flight, trilling as they do so. It is a plangent and evocative sound, one that used to echo from many a hillside at this time of year, but is now seldom heard.

2 APRIL

The bitter winter winds have now abated somewhat and the air has a fresher, less abrasive quality. In the adjacent valley I'm scanning the hill tops for the appearance of a scouting kite over its nest area and, as if on cue, one sails into view, its long wings flapping leisurely and its forked tail twisting to manoeuvre it with immaculate precision over the terrain. It floats gently down, almost vanishing as its mottled brown plumage merges with the dead bracken and desiccated grass of the hillside, landing in a large clump of oaks where it is lost in the web of branches. Three buzzards circle ever higher on the spring thermals, mewing gently. In the domain below, the smaller avian species pursue their daily routines too.

Coal tits, goldcrests and siskins forage communally in the Sitka spruces, calling to advertise their presence to potential competitors. Their plumage is fresh and colourful, signalling their peak condition.

Billowing cumulus piles over the hills on a cool blue backdrop. The valley imparts a tranquillity as if it is awaiting the burst of spring proper. Only the stream seems ignorant of the season's change and still careers along its deep-scarred course at frantic speed, noisily charging its way to the sea.

The squirrels have long past used up their winter stores and now come cheekily to the bird table to steal food, before scampering off into the hedge with nervously flicking tails.

Flocks of fieldfares and redwing are scouring the fields for seeds, building up energy for the flight North, as are groups of bramblings among the chaffinch flocks, some already in their summer finery of glossy blue-black and peach.

At night the calls of migrating waders echo eerily from the hills and their shadowy shapes flit past the pale clouds back-lit by a full moon. A solitary tawny owl hoots from the copse behind the house.

5 APRIL

The weather is warming up at last and the morning is dry and crisp. A ceramic blue sky is adorned with only a few static wisps of cloud, like dandelion seeds stuck to wet paint. Wood pigeons are cooing peacefully from the ivy-entwined ash and a blackbird in the crown is mellifluously voicing his territorial claims to the hedge adjoining the cart track. The butter-yellow celandines spangle the verge, alongside blooming snowdrops and nodding daffodils.

As the air absorbs the sun's heat, it creates thermals, loved by the bigger birds of prey. The kite pair, silent most of the time, are mewing from trees on opposite sides of the valley, like Swiss peasants yodeling to each other. A short while later they take to the air, utilising the thermals to circle up high together with three buzzards also enjoying the effortless uplift.

On the path my resident pair of pied wagtails run back and forth like clockwork, after the swarms of flies teased from their winter sleep by the sun's warmth and easier to catch here than in the long grass.

The buds on the trees are still firmly closed, not yet trusting the promise of this sudden warmth, but it can't be long now before they burst from their integuments. There is scarcely a breath of wind and the valley is still, but tense with a wound-up energy. Over the larch wood a male goshawk is circling tightly over what is probably his nesting tree. Smaller birds hide where they can. He then spirals slowly upwards until he looks as small and innocuous as a skylark, and then drifts out of sight, allowing the fugitives to emerge from hiding places and resume their lives.

6 APRIL

The warmth is wheedling the moisture from the soil and it is steaming up the hills. There are new-born lambs everywhere and their bleating resounds from every valley. They run after their mothers and head-butt their udders for milk. I relish the heat on my sun-starved skin and am forced to squint in the sharp, glinting light.

Although tempted to sunbathe and enjoy an inactive day, my Puritan conscience pricks lethargic limbs into action. I decide to explore the 'Goosander Valley', only a couple of miles to the North. I call it 'Goosander Valley' because it's where I saw my first goosander in mid-Wales. It is also a favoured area for kites and has, in some past years, held a peregrine eyrie. I wish to check whether it is still being occupied.

I begin my walk at a roadside church, surrounded by a dry-stone wall. It encloses a small, neat graveyard which, on reading the headstones, seems to belong solely to the Jenkinses and Joneses. Most of the graves are well cared for and decorated with fresh bouquets of wild flowers. A robin is singing his melancholic sub-song from a big yew.

The river has gouged a deep, steep-sided canyon. This has been colonised by birch and oak, which the years have encrusted with lichen. The trees grip the steep hillside tightly with their talon roots. Moss, heather and bilberry flourish between the short fossil-like trunks and exposed roots. The high, narrow and flinty path winds through the trees above the careering river below. Their new canopy forms a colander for the bright light which streams through the holes. As I cautiously pick my way along the narrow track, I dislodge a pebble, which gambols, tinkling down the bank hitting the water with a dull sploosh. Creating such a disturbance feels like a crass act of vandalism in these muted cloisters. I shrink from my own clumsiness.

A little further on, from below, I can hear a faint sound above the drone of the river. Now louder, this metallic call ricochets from the rocky banks and a dark brown thrush-like bird shoots downstream, landing on a boulder in the flood and begins displaying to its mate, which remains hidden from me.

The dipper cocks its tail and opens its trembling wings like an overgrown nestling begging for food, and performs this ritual for a few minutes, before shooting off out of sight.

The overhanging branches and twigs of the trees feather my face as I dive and duck beneath them, clutching at trunks to steady myself on the slippery path. I emerge from the wood to face a steep cliff and am greeted by the angry ear-splitting screams of the peregrine pair which have established their eyrie here. I don't wish to be the object of their ire for any length of time, so retreat back into the wood. On my return, a fluttering movement from the stream below catches my attention. My binoculars reveal a daffodil yellow and slate grey bird with a long, wagging tail. It hovers over the water, catches an insect and flies back to land on a stone in the stream; a little further down, its slightly duller mate is doing the same. Grey wagtails are perhaps the most characteristic birds of the Welsh streams and are always a joy to watch. They may stay around the rivers during the winter if the weather is very mild, but many move farther south, before returning again in spring.

Over the densely wooded slopes, a kite circles its territory and a pair of acrobatic ravens annoy a lumbering buzzard which is at their mercy. They behave like terriers worrying a cow, circling and diving in to snap at the slower bird. Only when the buzzard rolls on its back and shows its outstretched talons, do the ravens back off and leave it alone to continue its flight across the gorge.

As I leave the wood, a mouse-like bird catches my eye as it scampers up the trunk of a tall oak. It's probing the fissured bark with its curved stiletto beak, then sings its characteristic reedy tsee-tsee-tsee, before flying off to clamber up another tree trunk. Tree creepers are very much at home in these hanging oak woods where their insect food is plentiful.

I enjoy a late picnic lunch by the river, basking in the new spring warmth - wonderful after the long winter. The river bank has been dried by the sun and I sit on the grass watching the peat-coloured water rushing by and eat my sandwiches while listening to the bird song now filling the woodland glades. The deeper wheel ruts in the forestry track, shaded from the sun by the tall trees, are still filled with water from the recent heavy rains and large clumps of glutinous frog spawn shimmer just beneath the surface. The larch needles are just peeking lettuce-fresh from their scaly buds above my head, where a pair of coal tits are avidly searching for moth larvae.

7 APRIL

I have pin-pointed six peregrine eyries within a few miles of this valley. Unfortunately several of them are robbed each year, as the cliffs in mid-Wales are not too difficult for reasonably agile individuals to climb and some of the sites are easily discovered because they are quite accessible by road. If the birds are calling it is a give-away. Peregrines will return year after year to the same eyrie site and this makes it easy for nest robbers once they know the eyrie locations. Foreign falconers will pay big money for eggs or young.

The one I choose to visit today has been safe up to now. It is in a secluded valley, well away from the road and on a very steep cliff which would need good rock-climbing skills to scale. The crags are toothed and cracked and the rugged face rises to an awesome height.

The first wheatears are already re-colonising the mountain

sides and their pied rumps flash like diurnal glow worms as I disturb them from among the scree. Pipits too are returning to the moors and skylarks' songs cascade from the sky like refreshing showers of auditory rain.

I make a circumspect approach through a small plantation and as I emerge I can see two 'rocks' clearly silhouetted against the skyline. Through binoculars the 'rocks' mutate into peregrines - the tiercel and falcon are watching me closely. Their slate-grey backs merge with the rocks. Only their dark moustachial stripe, silvery eye and yellow cere on their beaks betray their animate reality.

The falcon sweeps off the hill, flies a wide circle around me, calling, warning me off. The way it flies, with unhurried determination and confidence, conveys its power. Its aerodynamic body of feathered steely sinew casts its shadow, racing over the ground like a freed soul. It knows it has no enemy to fear but man. So I descend to the bottom of the gorge and disappear around the cliff, away from their eyrie site to show that I mean no harm. I am more than happy to ascertain that they are still here and have not been robbed.

On the nearby reservoir two male and one female goldeneye, delaying their departure for the north, are swimming complacently on the flat leaden sheet of open water. Unlike the equivalent Scottish waters, Welsh upland lakes are puzzlingly devoid of bird life. A pair of sandpipers may breed or the odd mallard pair, but otherwise the lakes are usually deathly quiet. So to encounter these late goldeneyes here is as uplifting as unexpectedly meeting a friend in a cemetery.

As I walk down the slope back to the cottage a bullfinch pair seeks refuge in a dense hawthorn clump. Chiff-chaffs, too, have arrived in force and their bi-syllabic, repetitive song tinkles in the small larches. Further down, I spy a long tailed tit with a feather in its beak dive into some scraggy gorse bushes. I approach the spot cautiously and find a beautiful igloo-like, domed nest, built of moss and silver lichen and lined luxuriously with soft feathers. The bird's long tail protrudes from the entrance hole, as it arranges the lining. Long tailed tits have a predilection for thorn or gorse bushes because of the protection these afford from predators, like jays and magpies

The evening arrives too quickly. The sun ripens to a peachy orange orb as it sinks behind the gathering evening mists; the hills recede in pastel layers of pink, blue and pale violet, as in a Turner landscape. As the dusk is slowly cloaked by night, pipistrelle bats flicker around the cottage.

8 APRIL

Today is damp and cool, everywhere veiled in a fine mist. Cloud is rolling down the hills, like smoke from a battlefield. It is not much use venturing higher into the hills, so I stay in the low lying areas. From the river valley I catch a glimpse of a goshawk flying with strong, measured wing beats low over a bracken-covered slope to vanish in a fir wood. These large woodland hawks are not easy to see despite their size. They are very secretive apart from a very short period in the early part of the year when they often circle or indulge in courtship play above the nesting area. At other times they retreat into the extensive stretches of plantations, to emerge only for a quick kill. This bird probably has a nest nearby, as I've seen it on a number of occasions, but always only fleetingly.

I feel sure the birds of prey will have by now left the coast

Lapwings with young

along with the northwards migrating ducks and waders, but I decide to investigate nevertheless. I've no sooner begun to walk out over the mudflats when 30 or so lapwings suddenly rise as a female sparrowhawk glides low over them and is mobbed until it finds refuge in a clump of willows. So much for preconceptions! The lapwing continue swooping and gamboling over the damp fields, pee-whitting excitedly. Once so common, these farmland birds have become a rare species in many areas, driven out by sheep, modern agricultural processes and probably the predation of ever increasing crow and magpie populations. It is uplifting to see them again here. They are one of my most enduring boyhood memories, indelibly associated with early spring. Their pied and round-winged presence was a feature of most spring wheat fields and grasslands. I would often find their scrapes and admire their clutches of four camouflaged, mottled, pointed-end eggs. Their haunting calls characterised the countryside in spring as much as seed sowing and lambing.

By a small, shallow pool, I surprise three snipe avidly probing the soft edges. These are also birds which have become quite rare with the draining of wetlands and the increase in intensive farming. When I mount the dyke wall, revealing my full height, I startle a party of twenty redshank from the mud banks exposed by the retreating tide. Their shrill piping notes bounce along the length of the dyke.

Small groups of mallard, their curlicued tails and larger size distinguishing them from two pairs of teal, are feeding in a distant flooded field among the rushes, and three buzzards flap lazily over a flock of grazing sheep. Out on the salt flats small groups of what look like headless birds are in fact curlews asleep in the midday sun, their heads buried in their back plumage. A few desultory piping notes ring over the marsh from small numbers of oystercatchers. Far out on the estuary, shellduck and wigeon are 'nosing' through the soft mud and a flock of squawking, squabbling black headed gulls is mobbing five fishing mergansers over the open water. The shellduck will be the local breeding population that remain after their winter companions have left.

Walking back along the dyke my attention is drawn by anxious piping ahead. On a narrow shingle bank two oystercatchers are sitting. As I get closer, they stand up and wander away with feigned nonchalance. Their eggs are almost impossible to differentiate from the surrounding pebbles. Oystercatchers make no nest, just a shallow scrape. I leave rapidly to allow them to return before any lurking sharp-eyed crow can rob them.

There are still one or two winter migrants loitering on the estuary. A pair of elegant greenshanks are feeding on the muddy banks, and as I continue along the top of the dyke, enjoying the warmth of the late afternoon sun, I flush a dark bird with white rump and tail from the water's edge. It circles once, calling and then flies off over the marsh. It is a green sandpiper on the way to its Scandinavian breeding grounds.

Sedge warblers have also returned and are churring like badly tuned miniature motorbikes in the dense undergrowth by the track and a common whitethroat is delivering its rushed throaty little ditty from a bramble bush. The sinking sun has now suffused the dusk sky with a translucent pink and, as a clear signal of the approaching summer, my first swallow of the year flits buoyantly over the dyke, its plumage caught in an aureole of golden light. I smile contentedly to myself and muse about why I'm so happy. The predictable return of migrant birds and the certainty of the seasons' change are wonderfully reassuring factors in a too-rapidly mutating world.

These migrants come in waves and, like latecomers to a choir already in concert, add their voices almost unnoticed to the others. The garden warblers arrive after the blackcaps, swifts after swallows and martins, the spotted flycatcher behind the pied flycatchers and the latest, the nightjar, only arrives from mid-May to add his churring to the crepuscular evensong. They all find their way back from Africa with impeccable navigational skills, returning to the same valleys, hill slopes or hedgerows as the year before. If they find their habitat changed or indeed gone, they are forced to move on, to seek alternatives, if there are any. Some birds, like the red-backed shrike or wryneck simply gave up and rarely come anymore, others like the grasshopper warbler or yellow wagtail are reduced to a few small circumscribed areas.

12 APRIL

The night brought a heavy and continual downpour, but the dry peat soaks up the rain like a lover the longed-for words of endearment. By daybreak it has cleared and the air is now fresh and bright. I spend the morning putting up more nest boxes on several oaks in the wood. It is still not too late for tits to take possession and certainly early enough for pied flycatchers which haven't arrived back yet.

In between my hammer blows, a pair of goldcrests seep-seeps animatedly from the tops of the sibling firs next to the cottage and the oak wood echoes to the metallic chinking of great and blue tits, almost as if they are welcoming the supply of new homes.

The afternoon offers an opportunity to explore the river in the lower valley. It is in full spate, invigorated by the early spring rains. I follow the riverside track through a fir plantation and mixed woodland. The river at this point cascades in a series of cataracts, swirling eddies and foaming currents. The banks and trees here are rimed with a thick, furry coat of moss, and polypodium ferns sprout from branches and forks in the oaks. It is like wandering through a tropical rain forest, I certainly don't feel that I am in a British wood. The damp oozes from the luxuriant vegetation and my skin becomes clammy.

I disturb a fishing male goosander, hidden behind a bend in the river. He rises sharply from the water in a shuddering of spray and a threshing of wings, finds his height and flies straight but low, below the treeline, downstream. His velvet head, creamy breast and magpie wings flash against the dark trees. These beautiful sawbills are a relatively recent invader of mid-Wales and such large ducks appear somewhat incongruous in its narrow gorges and on its small streams. I feel they belong on the big lakes or wide estuaries. However they are a welcome addition to the limited fluvial fauna, although many a fisherman would disagree and argue that their presence depletes fish stocks. Despite their size and distinctive plumage markings, they can be surprisingly elusive, choosing to breed in narrow, tree-encrusted gorges which are difficult to reconnoitre.

A few days later, at around the same time, I return to this part of the river and wait quietly on the river bank, secreted behind thick brambles, to see if the goosander returns. I don't have to wait more than fifteen minutes, before I hear a beating of wings, followed by a splash as he skates to a stop and settles down in the olive water. His neck is stretched while he looks warily around before being assured that it is safe. I am motionless and he doesn't see me. Only a few minutes pass before he is joined by his mate. She lands alongside, exchanges a few low clucking notes with him and they both begin to preen. I feel like an interloper watching ritual nuptials at a forbidden and sacred place. They don't stay more than a few minutes, before swimming downstream out of my sight, no doubt to do some fishing.

I feel certain they must be nesting in the vicinity and I examine the riverside for nesting holes in the old oaks that fringe the river. I am only able to find one that looks remotely suitable, and as the hole is not very high, I clamber up the trunk which leans over the water, to take a peek while the birds are away. I'm almost knocked into the river by a large brown bird which emerges from the hole, to fly silently off into the tangle of alders. It is a tawny owl! In the capacious hollow I can discern two large, greenish-white eggs and one smaller, rounder white one. There is no doubt the owl has taken over the goosanders' hole and is now incubating their eggs and one of her own.

Normally I would not want to disturb the owl again, but this is so unusual and I'm really curious to know what will happen, so return once more the next day. I tap the bole of the oak gently with a stick and, on cue, the owl emerges and flies off on silent wings. When I examine the hole this time I am amazed to find two fluffy little goosander chicks. They couldn't have been more than a few hours old. They look like children's toys - furry, cuddly and dainty, and it saddens me to know that they will not be able to survive on a diet of dead voles. I have no wish to know the predictable outcome and don't return again.

13 APRIL

As so often in early spring, a few warm and balmy days do not necessarily presage the end of winter and today underlines the point with a vengeance. I awake to a Christmas card landscape. The whole valley is decked in a thick mantle of snow and frozen in awed silence. The newly arrived migrants must wonder if they've arrived in the wrong hemisphere. The cold, northern wind meeting the warmer Gulf Stream air has conspired to produce this unseasonal precipitation.

Tits are sparring hungrily over the nuts and crumbs I've put out on the terrace. The buzzards are scrutinising the snowy wastes with famished yearning from their lookout posts. New-born lambs, driven from the hills, huddle along the roadside verges. They look so fragile and vulnerable, but are from a hardy breed and most will survive almost anything the Welsh weather can throw at them. The ravens, too, are inured to this kind of weather and a nest in the local quarry already has two fully-fledged chicks. Ravens prefer inaccessible cliff refuges for their nests, but the scarcity of such sites in Mid-Wales leads many to utilise trees and on the moors even these can be in short supply. One year, I found a raven's nest in a stunted hawthorn, only two or three meters high - the only object above ground level for miles around. The nest, in the absence of readily available twigs, had been constructed largely of sheep bones collected from the moor. The female on the nest was quite a sight, sitting like an avian necromantic atop her charnel house of assorted jaw, pelvic and other bones.

14 APRIL

The night brings gale-force winds and driving rain following the snow. It is bitterly cold and I wonder how our migrants, their bodily reserves low after their long journeys, will survive. Unexpectedly, the morning brings sunny spells and the wind has dropped.

I decide to check how the two raven fledglings in the quarry are doing. The coming and going of workmen each day hasn't disturbed them, but have they survived the bad weather?

I'm shocked to see the ledge which held the big nest now ominously empty. Am I confused, have I got the wrong ledge?

No, the heavy splashes of excrement clearly mark where the nest once was. I have to investigate.

I climb the gate, irresponsibly ignoring its 'Hard hats must be worn' sign - but I don't have one with me - and walk up to the cliff face. There lying at the foot of the cliff is an enormous pile of sticks which had been the nest. Clearly the night's gales have brought it crashing down. You'd have needed more than a hard hat if that had landed on you. I begin to pull the sticks away to see if the young birds are trapped beneath. Underneath is the nest lining, a thick, matted blanket of sheep's wool, but no sign of the chicks. I'm wondering what might have happened to them when a loud angry croak, just above my head takes me by surprise. One of the adult ravens plunges towards me like an evil, winged goblin. At that moment, as I look up from the nest, I spot the two young ravens sitting silent and still on a grassy hummock, only a few feet from where I'm standing, as if pretending not to be there. They can't quite fly as yet and the grey shafts of their fledging tail and wing quills are still visible. They are wet and a little dishevelled, but otherwise unharmed. I leave the site quickly, feeling certain the adults will look after them even though they no longer have the protection of the nest.

16 APRIL

While taking an early morning stroll along the valley ridge, I spot Rusty, the female kite, as she sails into view below me, the pale creamy 'V' on her upper wings standing out in the bright light. She crosses the silvered serpent of the stream to settle on the branch of a dead beech. Shortly afterwards, Snowyhead, the male, follows her.

Birds of prey have incredible visual acuity, but spend most of their time scanning the ground below, not expecting either sources of food or of danger to come from above them. Because of this, from my elevated perch, I'm able to watch them both undetected.

Snowyhead glides towards her and then, with slowly undulating wings, mates with her, silently, as she rests on the branch. He then swoops down to take a stick and carries it to the nest in a tall beech close-by. A minute or so later, he proceeds to mate with her once more, as if to make sure, and again takes a stick to the nest, as if encouraging her to use the home he's built.

A pair of ravens nesting on the other side of the valley innocently drift into the kites' territory and Snowyhead is temporarily distracted from his amorous pursuits to dive-bomb them mercilessly, driving them back to their own side.

24 APRIL

The morning is warm and the sun is glowing in a cloudless sky. The mountains look as if draped in diaphanous veils, their usually harsh contours smudged into pale pastel tones by the diffuse light. Sand martins and house martins are swooping over the stream in welcome release from the inclement weather. The new warmth is bringing out clouds of midges and other insects – a vital food source for the spring migrants.

Although the chrome yellow celandines that have studded the verges for the past fortnight are now fading to a pale lemon, other flowers are beginning to replace them. Clusters of

WINGS OVER THE VALLEY

primroses shimmer from under the shading hedges, violets, like bright, inquisitive eyes, peer from among the grass stems, the alluring scent of the first bluebells is wafted up the lanes and new fern shoots are uncoiling like springs from the tangled rust of last year's fronds. From the alders by the brook, the newly arrived pied flycatchers are calling and grey wagtail pairs, too, are returning to the upland streams.

Behind the cottage, the Forestry Commission has clear-felled the firs, but presciently left a few tall rowans for tree pipits. Already four males are singing, their wheezy, high-pitched songs cascading over the hill as they twirl, parachuting down to land on the rowans. Our garden warbler has re-established his territory next to the cottage and is now singing with abandon. On the estuary, too, the handover is almost complete. The winter flocks of ducks and waders have repaired to their northern breeding sites, leaving the area vacant for the newcomers, which are losing no time in settling in. Two grasshopper warblers are reeling at each other in intense competition and a cuckoo announces his presence in echoing notes over the otherwise quiescent marsh.

White stars of water crowfoot with their shamrock-shaped leaves are covering the flood pools left by the early spring rains. Several whimbrel, the last of the migrant waders to pass through, are feeding there and are joined by three black-tailed godwits, already resplendent in summer plumage. Willow warblers dominate the soundscape in the willow scrub, supplemented by the melodious fluting of a lone blackcap.

Over the sea, small parties of 'comic' terns (it is impossible to discern whether they are common or arctic terns from this distance) are plunging for fish in the shallows, as they continue their flight northwards. A small flock of black-bellied dunlin whirls up from the shoreline and flies towards the estuary.

Further up-river a pair of goosanders is fishing. The river banks are aflame with gorse and among them greater stitchwort blossoms glint like scattered snow flakes around a blazing campfire. Peacock butterflies and some small meadow blues are fluttering over the array of blossom. I scan a large bank of shingle for nesting waders, but see nothing. I remain unconvinced and re-scan the area and, yes, one of the stones becomes animate, scampering like a mouse, dodging behind the larger ones. As I focus on it, it becomes a bird and I can pick out its dark crescented breast and eye band - it is indeed a little ringed plover. Then I discover its mate, barely visible behind the stones, as it makes its nest scrape. These birds rarely breed here, so I am excited to discover them. A shrill piping a little further along informs me that the common sandpipers have also returned and are marking out their riverbank territories.

The sun is still in the sky although it's after eight o'clock - one of the advantages of living close to the westerly extremity of Europe. I sit and relax after my walk, soaking up the sun's welcoming warmth, listening to the willow warbler singing with no signs of exhaustion and a redstart in the ash tree delivering its curt, throaty chaffinch-like song, bidding Helios farewell.

1 MAY

I look out of the window: It's cloudy, but shafts of light manage to penetrate the thin layers, providing succouring sunshine for the yearning vegetation. Overhead, high in the sky the first swifts are screaming.

Surprisingly a pair of pied flycatchers has taken possession of the box on the terrace which was occupied last year by bluetits. They haven't started building properly yet, although the female has brought in a few beak-fulls of moss. While the female is building, the male makes regular inspections of the box, as if to check his mate's nest building progress, but takes no part in the work.

While I am watching the pied flycatchers, a bluetit arrives and cheekily perches at the hole and actually enters the box. The pied flycatchers become very exercised about this and both alight on the low wall, close to the box, flicking their wings and tails, emitting angry 'ticking' notes. The female dive bombs the bluetit at the box, but it just ducks, like a clever boxer dodging badly-aimed blows, ignoring the attacks, and stubbornly carries on peeking into the box. The male flycatcher is a reluctant hero, he just sits and expresses his anger vocally. After a minute or so of this argument, the flycatchers appear to give up and fly off into the ash tree. The bluetit remains, enters the box again, but then also flies off. I wonder who will win this battle, although I would back the bluetit on the basis of these observations. However, much to my surprise the bluetit doesn't return, as if it's not interested. For several days the flycatchers seem to avoid the box too, but then the female continues building.

From a dependent branch of the fir tree next to the cottage a goldcrest's nest dangles like a diminutive hammock, only a foot or so above my head as I stand beneath. It is only visible as a dark cluster of moss among the needles. The female flutters anxiously close by, waiting for me to leave. I have heard the pair singing regularly in these trees and watched them feeding from the kitchen window while I breakfast, but I hadn't realised that they'd already built their nest. The male sings from the very top extremity of the fir: a high pitched, squeaky little song, ending in a short, rushed flourish of notes.

In the oakwood blue and great tits have taken possession of the boxes I've recently put up. The pied flycatchers seem to prefer the damper alder carr area by the stream. A bluetit, its bill packed with moss, like a green moustache, flies into one of the boxes in the oakwood. I watch it flitting back and forth with nest material. It is so intent on its task, that it doesn't even land on the perch, but flies straight through the aperture with unswerving accuracy. A great spotted woodpecker is drumming insistently from the upper part of the oak wood. He's always around, winter and summer, and makes his nest in one of the many oaks he can choose from.

2 MAY

As the weather grows steadily brighter, I decide to go to the coast to see how many seabirds have returned to their nesting ledges.

The steep cliffs rush down to meet the foaming sea. The gorse-covered slopes are ablaze with intense yellow blossom, wafting its heady coconut aroma into the warm air. The old stone walls and ledges are padded with pin cushions of pink thrift and delicate white campion bells, as transparent as rice paper. Among the gorse, patches of bluebells shimmer. The whole cliff top is a richly woven carpet of riotous colour. Far below, on a flat slab of rock, four seals are lazing in the sun. It takes me some time to realise they are there, because their grizzled elephantine skin blends perfectly with their rock bed. Apart from scarcely perceptible movement of their heads now and again, they remain absolutely immobile like old men enjoying an afternoon nap on the beach. Their glaucous eyes stare upward, but I'm uncertain whether they can see me. Their be-whiskered snouts are bathed by the lapping water.

A female merlin which has not yet returned to the moors, cruises past below me, like a brown leaf blown over an azure cloth. On the ledges, just above the breaking waves, dozens of pairs of guillemots and razorbills sit like dwarfs in evening dress at a tea party chattering animatedly. The guests keep leaving and arriving, others swim just offshore and are tossed like tiny pied corks. Their short stubby wings whirr rapidly as the birds fly the short distance from the sea up to their ledges . These wings are more useful as paddles when the birds are diving for fish, but in the air do not allow them much manoeuvrabilty - the sea is their true element.

Above the surging blue-green sea, gulls and kittiwakes wheel, their calls echoing off the rocky walls. A few grey fulmars circle effortlessly on stiff wings, letting the upward movement of air support them. A few snake-like, shags have also occupied several ledges and the sun brings out the green sheen on their backs and drying wings. From the narrow cliff-top path that follows an old stone wall, I flush a meadow pipit from its neat nest in a tussock of pink thrift. It contains four darkly freckled eggs. Above the gorse are dense swarms of tiny black, St. Mark's Flies, seemingly drugged by its heavy scent. They are providing a feast for the stonechats and whitethroats which are confused by the profusion and don't appear to know which to snap up first.

Whitethroats are furtive birds, and the one I'm watching dives into thick vegetation so that I can only follow its movements by the shaking umbels of cow parsley as it hops from stem to stem, hidden from view. A kestrel pair sails by on the lookout for unwary pipits or linnets feeding on the thrift-covered ledges. Before they disappear a splash in the water catches my eye and two bottle-nosed dolphins make a slow arc breaking the surface of the water. Like inseparable lovers, in perfect synchrony, they roll and play in the pellucid shallows for almost a quarter of an hour before sinking back and disappearing into the depths. These dolphins are a distinct sub-species peculiar to the Cardigan coast of Wales and can be seen regularly throughout the year off the coast.

On the billiard-table cliff top a pair of choughs are delving for succulent worms alongside three whimbrel. These diminutive curlews, with their distinctive dark 'eyebrows' and fluting call, are one of the latest of the Arctic breeding birds to pass through the area.

Almost all our own summer migrants have now returned and are busy re-establishing their territories. The pied flycatchers' mournful little three note song now tinkles from the woods and thickets. The Germans actually call these birds 'Trauerschnäpper' (mourning flycatcher), no doubt because of the male's funereal-looking plumage. The rusty-red tails of redstarts flash from the hedgerows as they fly off. In rough wetland areas the rasping twitter of whinchats emanates from the brown sedge. The speckled brown male with his elegant dark brown ear coverts, surmounted by creamy eyebrows can often be seen atop a dry stem or on an old teasel head in rough wetland or on bracken-covered slopes.

The birds' plumage at this time of the year has a bright healthy sheen to it: the light glances off the sleek black velvet of the great tits' caps, the caerulean of the blue tits glimmers as they bob about in the hedgerow and the ubiquitous magpies flaunt their prismatic tails.

The valley stream, which has its source on the hill at the top of the valley, has eroded the banks above the lead mine and the sheer sides offer half a dozen sand martins ideal nesting sites. These dusky little boomerangs sail down stream, then curve back and swoop up to hang at their holes, then let loose and repeat the manoeuvre.

All the peregrine pairs in the vicinity are now fully established at their eyries. The male of the pair usually acts as sentry on a rocky outcrop, close to its sitting mate, from where it can keep the surrounding country under surveillance and warn her in good time of approaching dangers.

At one site, close to a nearby country road, the birds use a plucking rock not far from the eyrie. I came across this one while walking on the hills earlier in the year. They bring their prey here to devour it in peace and quiet. It is adorned with a loose garland of jay and crow feathers which flutter in the slight breeze. I know several of these plucking rocks and I'm always fascinated to discover what birds the peregrines are taking by exmaining the feathers - sometimes red grouse, gulls or a magpie.

The birds are again using the eyrie from the previous year - peregrines will return year after year to the same site, if not robbed or harassed too much. Here in mid-Wales the mountains are not very high and suitable cliff faces, essential for peregrines, are at a premium.

This site is at the top of a steepish, scree-covered hill. The nesting ledge is on the bare face, but surrounded by small rowans growing out of fissures in the rock and by clumps of bilberrry and heather. I keep well away from it during the breeding season and content myself with watching the birds from a distance, but last year, once the young eyasses had flown, I climbed up to examine the eyrie. They had used an old raven's nest and the rim was decorated with a dozen or more pinky-red pigeon legs, some with their marking rings still attached. I was just glad no pigeon fancier could see this - it would convince him more than ever that peregrines are his worst enemy. Of course, the peregrine isn't necessarily partial to racing pigeons, but I've often seen flocks of them funneling through the valley and then circling in seeming confusion, attempting to find their orientation again. No peregrine is going to just sit there and watch this proffered meal pass in front of its eyes without attempting a stoop.

3 MAY

A clear, cloudless day, almost wind still.

Above the steep river valley a pair of kites is circling tightly over their nest site in the hanging oak wood. Redstarts and pied flycatchers are flickering everywhere. Near one of the many abandoned lead mines, I come across a female black redstart which is quite a rarity, as they don't nest in mid-Wales. An old lead mine seemed so appropriate for it, with its lead-grey plumage and quiet, unassuming behaviour.

The upper valley, only recently as quiet as a deserted ship, has now regained its fugitive population. From the oak wood I can hear a hammering and tapping. I follow the direction it's coming from and find myself standing under a tall oak, which appears to be the source of the sound. From a cleanly carpentered hole high up on the trunk, a sharp beak-chisel emerges, followed by a zebra-like head with red-rimmed eye and crimson nape of a great spotted woodpecker. I keep absolutely still. It looks around quickly, is reassured and returns to its woodwork. It keeps at it for about ten minutes, before leaving with its characteristic undulating flight, for a rest or some food.

The upper lakes are not quite as still and quiet now as they were. Over the first one I see my first house martins flicking over the water and a single swift scything the crisp air.

A cuckoo, that symbolic herald of summer, calls seductively from a hawthorn bush, but is mobbed by the resident tree pipit which forces it to flee across the valley. Its hawk-like shape, grey back and vermiculated breast, give it a strong ressemblence to a slow sparrowhawk. The tree pipit then resumes his paragliding, territorial display, flying steeply upward from his bush and spiraling down in song, to land gently on the same bush.

The birch buds have just broken and where the trees are numerous, their new foliage drapes the bracken-brown hills with delicate green tracery.

4 MAY

I awake to find a ground frost wintering the lower valley, but the sky is bright and clear, making the ice crystals on the grass stems sparkle. The frost, though, is rapidly melted by the rising sun.

Despite the early frost, I decide to venture on to the high peak which rises to over 700 metres. On peaks like this one, covered in scree and several species of alpine plants, it is usually possible, at this time of the year, to encounter a small trip of dotterel on their way north to their nesting sites in Scotland.

It is much colder up here, despite the sun, and a few flurries of unseasonable snow underline the difference in temperature only a few hundred meters above sea level can

Dotterel

make. From here I can see for fifty miles or so, all around. To the west, lies the sea, and where it breaks on the shore a thin thread of foam marks it off from a necklace of white-washed houses.

In a grassy tussock, next to a patch of bare scree, a skylark flutters off its nest containing three eggs. But I catch not even a glimpse of dotterel. They are among our latest arriving summer migrants, stopping off on their way north to rest on some of the most inhospitable peaks, where snow and ice, even in May, are far from unusual. They get their name from choosing such 'crazy' places and from their 'dotty' behaviour, allowing humans to approach quite close or even touch them on the nest. Despite their distinctive plumage, their chestnut breast and long, white supercillium, they are easily missed. You can walk within a few yards of them and not notice. A hill walker I meet informs me that he has seen a pair only a minute before I arrived.

As I descend, following the bed of a small stream, I come across a crow's nest in a small birch, growing in the stream bed. I can look into it from the high bank and see four bluey-green eggs. The bird watches me from a rocky outcrop close by and croaks angrily until I am well out of the way.

I come out onto a promontory where the bilberry is thick and in full bloom. Bees are humming hungrily around its myriad small pink bell flowers, collecting its unique nectar. Below me stretches a large spruce and larch plantation along a wide valley. As I look down enjoying the long view, a female goshawk appears from one end and begins circling the wood. It doesn't see me for some time, because I am standing above it. I admire its strong, broad wings and, through binoculars, I can discern its yellow-ringed, keen-as-a-dagger eye below a white supercilium. It sees me almost immediately and as we make eye contact it dives at breakneck speed into the firs, to vanish from my sight.

In one of the larches on the lower hillside, where the wood is less densely planted, I spot an enormous bedstead of a nest. I think it may be a goshawk's. I don't wish to disturb it, so I approach from higher up, through the wood, from where, using binoculars, I can look down on top of it. I am surprised to see a brown, banded tail and rounded head protruding above the nest rim. The bird's eyes are almost closed, as if it is half asleep. Its bushy 'eyebrows' and pale earthenware colour provide me with incontrovertible evidence that I am indeed looking at a tawny owl. These birds usually nest in tree holes, but such holes are at a premium here, where most of the trees are too slender, so this one has chosen what is probably an old buzzard's nest to make its own. As I watch it, an anxious seep seep close by reveals a willow warbler's tiny, domed nest in the damp grassy bank on which I am sitting. It has six ginger-freckled eggs, each no bigger than the nail on my little finger. I retire quickly so that the bird can return to its nest.

Evening slowly quietens the songsters and the crow's wing of night brushes the scurrying remnants of light from the hill tops, plunging the valley into blindness, where sounds take on a new meaning, become magnified and spectral. As if to underline this, a tawny owl gives a muted hoot from the lower valley and brittle, scurrying sounds can be heard from the wood.

5 MAY

I take an early walk to the upper lakes again. The low, morning sun is blinding in its intensity and it turns the dew-soaked grass into spears of sparkling diamonds. It was only a few days ago that I'd put up new bird boxes around the cottage but already proprietal behaviour has been adopted. A male pied flycatcher perches on a hazel, close to the one on an alder by the stream. It clicks angrily, flicking its wings and tail, and waits until I depart.

The long tailed tit is now sitting on its eggs in the gorse bush, its long tail protruding from the nest hole, like a flag on its pole denoting residence. A scattering of what look like blue crystals in the grass, are revealed on closer inspection to be violets flowering beneath the gorse, all along the bank of the stream.

An angry cawing pulls my eyes to the sky where the buzzard, mercilessly harassed by a pair of crows is attempting to traverse the valley to its nest in the larch wood. I feel sorry for these birds, because they are always being attacked and worried by crows or ravens, like the fat boy at school tormented by more agile youngsters, unable to escape or retaliate because of his bulk. Eventually the buzzard reaches the safety of the wood and the crows call off their attack.

The lakes, so recently deserted have now become the focus of avian attention. Two herons are strutting about in the bulrushes, several pairs of mallard are sun bathing on the shore, a pied wagtail is rushing dementedly back and forth confused by the swarms of midges, swallows and sand martins are skimming the surface, gorging on the sudden eruption of insects.

A pair of common sandpipers, like two over-excited adolescents, are display chasing low over the water, their stiff wings forming double arcs with their reflections in the unruffled water. Landing on the far side, they trill with abandon.

Snowyhead, the kite, flies slowly up from the valley, curious to know what I am up to. He watches me closely as I walk down the lane, flying parallel with me and then lands in a large ash on the hillside, not too far from his nest. From there he keeps an eye on me until I retreat down the valley.

Two skylarks are in full-throated voice high in the sky and a female whinchat sings from a dwarf willow in the low swampy patch between the two lakes. Several wheatears forage among the dry, stony patches and a bright yellow hammer sings his 'little bit of bread and nooooo cheese' ditty from atop a hawthorn. In the remnants of gorse scrub, inexplicably left by the farmer who cleared the whole hillside of it, a small party of twittering linnets takes possession, their breasts glowing brightly in the sun as if set on fire by the flickering yellow flames of gorse.

6 MAY

This morning, taking an early walk through a young larch plantation above the valley, I disturb a large hare from its bed in the long grass, sending it bounding off down the slope, its long, soot-fringed ears erect as it runs. They are not a common sight in these hills, but a few pairs manage to survive predation by foxes.

An aristocratic-looking buzzard, new to the area, arrives in the narrow neck of the valley behind the cottage, close to where the resident buzzard is nesting. He lands in an ash below me and I can observe him at my leisure. He looks more like an osprey than buzzard, with magnificent snowy plumage with only one or two darker striations, his liquescent eyes studying the ground below him. He stays only an hour and then disappears. I haven't seen him since.

A pair of stonechats are nesting in the gorse on the top of the ridge and their hard pebble-tapping notes carry far over the valley.

A peregrine appears from nowhere, dropping like a sliver of blue slate from the sky. It curves over the oaks, and as it whooshes past me I look into its dark eye, enclosed by its moustachial stripe. In seconds this sleek projectile is gone, like a meteorite. You wonder shortly afterwards whether you actually witnessed it or simply imagined it - the sky is again empty and from a tree nearby a redstart continues singing blissfully unaware of the shadow of death passing so close.

Most birds now have eggs, apart from the few latecomers. In my bird box on the birch tree behind the cottage a bluetit is sitting on 10 finely freckled eggs. From the bank bordering the lane I flush a meadow pipit as I walk past. Closely examining the bilberry clump from whence she flew, I discover a carefully woven nest, lined with hair and cradling four densely speckled chocolate-coloured eggs, the bilberry fronds protecting it like the eyelid an eyeball.

A sparrowhawk flies overhead, carrying prey which slows it down and makes its wing beats laboured. It either doesn't see me or ignores me, flying low, straight ahead to its nest in the larch plantation. My curiosity aroused, I decide to investigate more closely.

As I enter the dense wood, it reverberates to the unmistakable screams of sparrowhawks. I can't see them through the thick weave of twigs, but they must be close, judging by the volume of their sound. I imagine the chicks must have hatched and my presence alarms them, because they are usually silent when they have eggs. Close to where they are making such a fuss, there is a narrow ride where the trees have been felled and here two of the stumps have been used as plucking places. Around one I find the red, black and white feathers of a great spotted woodpecker and at the other song-thrush plumage. In this dimly lit, claustral wood, before these sacrificial altars, scolded by screaming voices, I feel I have intruded into some sacrosanct place of ritual, where my presence is an affront to the high priests. I leave quietly and with due reverence to rejoin the forestry path.

While I'm passing a broad marshy area I hear the

unmistakable reeling churr of grasshopper warblers from dense sedge, I can distinguish three separate birds reeling at each other. I walk towards one of them and creep very close, but it stops 'singing' abruptly. I wait hoping to see the bird but nothing moves. Then the reeling starts up again to my left. I walk in that direction and the same thing happens - the reeling stops and I see nothing, then the reeling begins again behind me. Grasshopper warblers are magicians of the vanishing act. They are very reluctant to fly, preferring to creep through the thick vegetation unseen and only their voices reveal their presence. They are able to settle in this spot because sheep have been excluded from the marsh, leaving its rough vegetation undisturbed.

7 MAY

To be in a hanging oakwood on a sun-drenched day is like being in a modern, airy concert hall and to enjoy the sense of space, light and acoustics. It contrasts starkly to the experience in the fir plantations which are dark and frigidly silent, reminiscent of a gothic cathedral with their strict verticals and ascetic bareness.

It is fascinating to note the differences in the bird life between fir and deciduous woods, although some birds appear perfectly at home in either. Wrens, robins, song thrushes and chaffinches for instance are found almost equally in both. The fir woods though are the true home of goldcrests, siskins, crossbills and coal tits and these are seldom seen or heard in deciduous woods. Pied flycatchers, redstarts, blue and great tits as well as the warblers, on the other hand, are domiciled in the deciduous woodlands, although chiffchaffs, willow warblers and even the odd wood warbler can be found on the fringes of fir woods.

Today is again unbearably hot, the incandescent sun scorching the unwary. The sheep huddle under the little shade they are able to find and many birds seem to have lost the energy to sing.

I decide to keep to the woodland shade and investigate the local arboreal bird life. I begin near the stream in the lower valley, where it is damp and cool under the alders and oaks. A cuckoo is calling from the hillside, its soft bitonal note carrying far into the valley.

Light splashes generously through the canopy allowing good ground vegetation to flourish. A wood warbler trills its short glissando as it falls gently like a yellow oak leaf to a lower branch. I encounter pied flycatchers at regular intervals as I follow a sheep track up through the hanging oaks. They are not easy to see in the shimmering foliage which is now quite dense, but their short penetrating song is unmistakable. Redstarts, too, are singing from the higher canopy and occasionally I catch a flash of a henna-coloured tail as they fly from one perch to another. Blue tits and great tits are in abundance and are avidly searching the foliage for juicy larvae to feed their usually numerous broods. A great spotted woodpecker 'chuck-chucks' at me with annoyance from its cleanly chiseled nesting hole. Warblers populate the glades, where there is bramble and honeysuckle undergrowth, but they only come into full song as the sun's heat subsides in late afternoon. Willow warblers are singing in all the more open woodlands. Their almost whispered little song gives the impression of diffidence, so unlike the macho song of the garden warbler which loudly proclaims: I'm back, listen to me! A male blackcap gives a coloratura performance from an exposed branch. His beak is agape and his whole body is trembling with the effort of projection, determined to make sure his voice carries as far as possible.

As I cross a bracken-covered glade, a tree pipit floats from the sky on extended wings, twirling like a large sycamore seed, whistling his seep-seep song to draw the attention of prospective mates. This summer visitor is found widely on open, bracken-covered areas or on felled-woodland.

The fir wood is densely planted, allowing no light to penetrate and there is therefore no ground vegetation except at the edges. Such woodlands are the valleys' equivalent of Trappist monasteries. Even my footsteps are silent on the needle-strewn ground. There is only the faint but persistent whispering of goldcrests high up in the crowns and the occasional drawn-out nasal wheezing of a siskin. Then, in rebellious disobedience to the rules, a wren close by bursts into a loud trilling that shatters the tranquillity. It dashes off and lands on the root plate of a wind-blown spruce, disappearing into the tangle of roots and moss. I follow it, curious to discover where it went. As I bend to examine the underside of the torn roots, the small bird shoots out under my nose and scolds me loudly from a nearby bramble thicket. It has emerged from a small hole in a tiny, compact globe of moss and dry bracken which is embedded in the roots and earth of the ripped-up tree. Perfectly camouflaged and only recognisable as a nest, when I'm inches from it. I realise how appropriate is the wren's scientific name, troglodytes, meaning cave-dweller.

It is now the height of the breeding season and almost every suitable habitat has its nesting birds. The present warm spell will be valuable for their success, by bringing forth a profusion of insects and allowing vulnerable fledglings to put on weight and protective plumage before the next spell of cold and wet weather arrives. In many years April and May can be very cold and wet in these valleys and lead to heavy losses of nests and young birds, particularly of ground nesting ones like willow and wood warbler.

I come out of the fir wood into the brightness as if emerging from a wine vault into the light of day, quite chilled and pleased to feel the warmth of the sun on my face again. At the edge of the wood I disturb a sun-bathing slow-worm, which shuffles off slowly to disappear in the tangle of long grass.

9 MAY

Earlier in the year I'd heard a goshawk calling from one of the lower valley woods. I'd also spotted a male circling tightly over the larches one early, sunny morning.

I hadn't seen the birds since, but know they should be nesting by now, so decide to see if I can locate the spot.

It is a dry cloudy day but the ground is still moist from the recent heavy rain. As I enter the wood along a small forestry track, I'm greeted by a medley of bird song: blue and great tits, willow and wood warblers, blackcaps and garden warblers. It is difficult to separate out the individual songs from the complex symphony of sound.

I've hardly walked a few meters along the path when a small mouse-brown bird with a 'black beret' flutters from a tangle of honeysuckle at the path side and tuk-tuk-tuks at me from the scrub. I peer into the honeysuckle and discover a small, neatly woven, but fragile nest of dry grass stems. Within its deep cup lie five olive-mottled eggs. The nest is so thin, I can see the ground through its loose weave. What an example of architectural skill to construct such an apparently flimsy structure which is nevertheless strong enough to hold eggs and later young birds as well as to survive the buffeting of wind and rain. It is a blackcap's nest and, exceptionally here it is the male which is brooding.

The tall and slender beeches are just breaking into leaf and look as if they have been planted on a beach: the flat, sand-coloured leaf litter is interrupted only by dazzling azure pools of bluebells. The air is heavy with their wild hyacinth scent. The larches hide pairs of whispering goldcrests and seeping coal tits. In one of them, on the slope below me, I can just discern a very large nest in a fork. The thick mattress of sticks could be the goshawk's nest I seek. I raise my binoculars with excitement. There is indeed a large bird sitting on the nest but it is not a goshawk. The nest is at the edge of the wood and the bird has its back to me, its attention focused on the open farmland stretching out below it. Its chocolate mottled back reveals it to be a buzzard. As it turns its head, the liquid pool of its eye flickers as it stares up at me, its short sharp beak and sturdy head silhouetted against the intense green of the field. It doesn't fly, but observes me warily until I walk on.

On the brow of the wooded hill, where the firs are only a year or two old and are interspersed with birch scrub, one garden warbler after another is singing in intense competition. Although the habitats of garden warblers and blackcaps overlap and their songs can be infuriatingly similar, the garden warbler is found at higher altitudes than blackcaps, which prefer the damper, shadier valley bottoms.

Despite my quartering the wood in all directions, the goshawks, if they are here, remain hidden.

I take the small road out of the wood that follows the river to the head of a contiguous valley. At the top, the river has carved a steep-sided narrow gorge in the rock and two years ago it held a peregrine's eyrie. It was robbed and the pair hasn't nested since. I position myself among a clump of Norway Spruces and scan the cliff through the curtaining branches. Near the top, on a grassy ledge, I'm overjoyed to see a white-throated, dark-moustachioed face staring at me. A robust peregrine falcon is sitting on its eyrie and keeping its all-seeing eyes on me. The pair has returned after a long absence and will hopefully be more successful this year, although I'm sceptical. It has been raided in the past and being so close to the road and just opposite a layby, it is not an ideal situation. To ensure its survival would involve a round-the-clock vigil for weeks on end, something I can't do, but I'm determined to monitor its progress as regularly as I can. It's an almost hopeless task to protect such birds' nests when you are up against extremely sophisticated criminals. In this case, only the birds' own efforts will allow them to survive.

As dusk slinks between the trees, I descend the wooded hillside to return home. On passing a rocky outcrop I am ambushed by a large bird, swooping down from a ledge above me and then sailing over the spires of the spruces. I can discern a strong muscular body and slender wings but in the half light and from behind it, I can't recognise what it is. Only as it turns and I see its side silhouette, its long tail, broad, strong wings and sharp-beaked head extended in angry surprise, do I realise it is a female goshawk. I'm not sure who's the most surprised, her or me. It was obviously roosting on the rock face for the night and I've inadvertently disturbed it. The bird circles twice and then glides off down the valley to be swallowed by the gathering twilight. My search had not been in vain after all - the goshawks are still around.

I follow its direction and as I reach the bridge crossing the river in the valley bottom, find myself surrounded by bats, skimming the trees and darting low over the river, in search of insects on the wing.

10 MAY

The oaks are in full leaf but the foliage is still tender and translucent, allowing the light to reach the heather growing beneath. The narrow path takes me along slopes thickly matted with bilberry which grows profusely before the foliage gradually occludes the light in late Spring. However, the bilberry here rarely flowers or bears fruit because it receives little sunlight once the trees are fully leaved.

I look up and see a kite. I follow it as it sails across the leaf-fringed pools of sky. It will have a nest in one of the oaks on the steep slope and is no doubt curious to see what I'm doing in its territory.

Pied flycatchers and redstarts serenade me from the shimmering green canopy and the treble tremolo of the wood warbler battles to be heard above the continuo of the river's baritone. Pillows of soft moss adorn the rocky ledges. A bonsai-like rhododendron is growing from a rock in mid-stream and its purple blossoms splash their luminous colour on the dark, peaty waters flowing beneath.

A sheep carcass, brought down by the Spring flood waters has become wedged between some rocks and a buzzard is gorging its fill on the foetid flesh. Further along, I spot a small peat-brown bird darting upstream on invisible wings - a dipper seeking a new feeding place. As it flies over the lichen-encrusted rocks it passes a flicker of pollen-yellow, blue and white which condenses into a grey wagtail chasing flies over the foaming, rushing current.

After half an hour's walk I come out of the wood onto open hillside, thick with heather. In front of me is a small cliff where peregrines once bred a year or two back. I check every year to see if they have returned, but the cackle of jackdaws as they flutter from the ledges tells me they have not. A fine drizzle begins and sends me scurrying back through the wood.

Even in May many days can be grey and drizzly, when the valley can seem almost like a prison and I find myself continually looking upwards for even a small window of blue. I console myself by reflecting that this part of the country would not be so green and luxuriant without its copious rain and it would also be more popular with intrusive holiday-makers if the weather were more clement.

11 MAY

Heavy rain falls during the night and the morning brings little promise of betterment. On the horizon, grey layers of mountains merge into the grey layers of cloud. The wind blows unremittingly from the North, bringing back Winter temperatures.

I return to the 'goshawk wood', still intrigued by the mystery of their disappearance. This time I enter by a different route and find myself walking along a very narrow, obviously rarely used track, alongside a stand of mature larches. Just around a bend of the track, in one of the larches I see an enormous, untidy mound of sticks and twigs. It looks like an old raven's nest. As I draw close and look up underneath it, I can make out a tail protruding over the rim. I tingle with excitement. Is this what I've been looking for? As I pause, she stands on the nest, showing her magnificent grandeur for a few seconds only before slipping off and vanishing in the green draperies of the larches. I'm thrilled to have located the goshawk's nest and know I've become party to a well-kept secret. Although goshawks are big birds and their nests are even bigger, they are notoriously difficult to watch. They nest deep in the evergreen forests, off the beaten track and avoid the vicinities of human habitation - the source of their original persecution and extinction in the British isles, before escaped hawking birds bred and formed the basis of a new stock.

In the early evening a charm of six goldfinches, together with a pair of siskins descend from the sky into the field outside my window. They feed avidly on the dandelion clocks. It looks so amusing because I can only see their small crimson faces peeking above the thick grass, like cheeky ruddy-faced children playing hide and seek.

13 MAY

The night stays clear and a full moon, its craters clearly visible through binoculars, shines into the bedroom window like a searchlight and the resident tawny owl emits a few desultory hoots from the big ash in the lane. Well before daybreak I am out of bed and drive a few miles further north, where the mountains are grander and there is more heather on the slopes. I'm hoping to locate a few pairs of the rapidly declining black grouse.

There are only a few birds left in mid-Wales now and they are very difficult to track down. The shrinkage of heather by intensive sheep farming has no doubt been one of the main reasons for their disappearance, but other factors will have played a part. In spring the males, the blackcocks, gather in small groups to 'lek'. This involves a complicated ritual of dancing and pouting with erect tails and puffed up breast feathers, while making deep bubbling sounds which carry over the valleys. This is done to impress the females who gather around the edge of the 'dance floor' and watch. To see and hear this pre-mating behaviour entails an early rise, before dawn and then often long, cold vigils in likely places. This year I'm lucky. I drive to an area of young plantation with good coverage of heather and bilberry - the sort of place the grouse would choose. I park on a forestry path and walk up onto a hill which gives me a wide view. The ground is soaking with dew and stars are still glittering in the sky, but already some birds are awake - a chiffchaff, a chaffinch and a robin are calling diffidently. I wait for perhaps half an hour as the sky slowly fills with pale light as if someone is turning the dimmer switch in the reverse direction. Then quietly at first, then louder, I hear the unmistakable 'bubbling' of blackcock from the opposite hillside. Through binoculars I can distinguish three males, their lyre like tails held erect by the white undertail coverts, their crimson wattles visible on their black heads, and their neck feathers distended, like prize fighters flexing their muscles. They move around each other as if unsure who will throw the first punch. A solitary female stands on the sidelines watching.

The light is becoming brighter by the minute and the rest of the bird world is waking. Suddenly, before I can fully appreciate what is happening, a female goshawk plunges through a gap in the small firs and catches one of the lekking grouse in its sharp talons, before the victim even realises an attack has been launched. The other three whirr off over the heather clumps, clucking with fear. The plump bird is dead within a few seconds, its heart punctured by the goshawks long claws. It feeds its fill on the ground, ripping away the black breast feathers and tearing chunks from the breast flesh. During feeding it remains alert, its vicious, yellow-ringed eyes scanning the surroundings between each gulp of meat.

I had been keen to become acquainted with goshawks, but not in this unexpected manner. Adult black grouse have few enemies apart from foxes and mankind, but the success of the goshawk in recent years is posing a severe threat to the few remaining pairs in this part of Wales, particularly during lekking, when the males are highly visible, sexually excited and off guard.

I leave this sad spot with mixed feelings of elation at having found lekking grouse and even of witnessing such a dramatic event, but saddened too by nature's own unwitting conspiracy in hastening the demise of certain species. As I tramp wearily back through the deep heather, my attention is caught by a large, grey ghost of a bird which appears floating like a pale piece of fabric against the dark backdrop of the heather moor. It flaps with slow, measured wing beats, low over the ground. It is completely ash-grey, apart from black-tipped primaries – a male hen harrier. As it approaches a small hill, it is suddenly dive-bombed by a single raven, which seems to take it by complete surprise, making it abruptly swerve in its flight. The raven swoops again and forces the much larger bird down on to the heather, where it lies spread-eagled for a second, wondering what has happened, before escaping across the moor. This bird, too, as beautiful and fascinating though it is, is not averse to taking young grouse as part of its diet.

17 MAY

This pass is an example of the Welsh countryside at its wildest. Crags protrude like jagged incisors into the gaping maw of the evening sky. The main cliff is like a giant unscalable fortress wall, over 30 metres high. It is forbidding and perilous in its awesome stature and the perfect setting for a peregrine eyrie. The bird's rasping call echoes menacingly from the face. But despite my scanning its ledges and crannies with binoculars, the bird remains hidden. The cliff miniatures everything around it. The broad valley, surrounding hills and woods stretch away from it, as if viewed through a wide-angled lens. Suddenly the bird flies, sweeping down off one of the ledges and becomes visible in movement.

I think I can hear a snatch of a ring ouzel's song from high up on the cliff, but am not sure. Whatever bird it is, it remains hidden on that impenetrable face.

18 MAY

Nightjars can only be heard and seen at dusk unless unwittingly disturbed while asleep during the day. At twilight the bird awakes to hunt moths and other nocturnal insects during the night, returning to its roost on a dead branch or fallen tree trunk where it will pass the diurnal hours. It is a very rare bird in this area. In fact it was totally absent for many years and only recently have a few pairs returned, drawn by the new felled-forest habitats.

After dinner, I go up into the hills a few miles from the cottage, where a substantial area of felled fir wood offers ideal conditions. Nightjars are probably the latest of our summer migrants to return and I calculate that they should have just about arrived.

I reach the plateau in time to be presented with a magnificent sunset, the kind one can see only on the West coast. The rose-red orb of the setting sun slips down behind the mountain ridge, leaving a warm afterglow. The pink-smudged twilight sky rests delicately on its pinnacled bed of dark firs and in perfect mimicry is inverted in the tranquil lake. Only the small trout nosing the surface for flies, disturb the surface momentarily. Willow warblers and goldcrests whisper into sleep.

The edges of trees and hills become ragged, the eye strains to make out detail, night slowly encircles, robbing my space. Nature unconsciously imitates gothic splendour with an array of tall, filigree spires silhouetted on the skyline against the stained-glass window of a frameless sky. The scribble of river far below, like a silver clasp decorates the slender neck of the dusky valley. As the indigo of night seeps in from the edges bird song ceases. A robin tinkles into silence and a mistle thrush flutes two last notes before retiring.

My sensory reliance shifts from my eyes to my ears. As the diurnal sounds subside, the nocturnal ones take on a larger significance. Every rustle, each distant hoot, howl or timid squeal forms an aural picture in my mind. Sounds are the signposts of night, giving you positions, distances, defining landscapes and activities. A breaking twig signals the descent of a large hare from the thicket above me. It hops down onto the forestry track and either doesn't see or smell me or chooses to ignore my presence. Hares are rarely hunted here and it has quite probably lost much of its fear of humans. It scampers at a leisurely pace down the track like a small kangaroo, stopping every so often to stand erect on its hind legs to listen, before hopping further, sniffing the ground as it does so. Its white scut stands out like a frost-covered teasel in the darkness. Another hare comes from the opposite direction, hops around me and wanders off into the trees.

Only about a quarter of an hour after the sun has set, I hear what I've come for: the soft, purring of a nightjar! It sounds rather like the incessant fluttering of a moth against a lamp shade. The birds can keep churring for up to an hour at a time and the sound carries for almost a mile on still nights. It emanates from a young plantation, but I can see nothing. I tiptoe towards the sound. It suddenly stops and a bird takes off from a small larch, flying upwards, with falcon-like slender wings and long tail, revealing why it is also known colloquially as the 'night hawk'. What a tremendous thrill to see and hear this most mystical of birds and to know it is now breeding in the area. One of its ancient names is 'goatsucker' which locals gave it because they thought it sucked the milk of goats during the night.

It's plumage is superbly camouflaged so that it remains virtually invisible during the day on the ground or on a dead branch. It is perfectly adapted to hunting at night. Its rictus has evolved to suit its diet of nocturnal insects; the fine hairs around its small beak, allow it, while on the wing, to sense moths and take them into its wide gape. It flies fast and silently, zig-zagging over the tree tops towards a small lake, where insects will abound and be easier to distinguish against the reflecting surface of the water.

Two tawny owls are calling each other from the valley below, their calls echoing eerily through the cool night air. I walk slowly back along the path, overtaking a hedgehog noisily nosing along the edge. Then a few hundred yards further on a badger, like a drunk returning home, crashes through the undergrowth, crosses the path in front of me to disappear on the other side, but I can hear it long after its white stripes have been erased by the night.

Bats swoop on translucent wings down the path, chasing the moths and midges. Twilight has now become impenetrable night. I am unlikely to see much more of the nightjar and am already shivering as the temperature drops rapidly at this altitude, so I retreat to the valley where a few pinpricks of light flicker enticingly far below.

25 MAY

There is no need of an alarm clock once the summer visitors are back. You are awoken by a chorus of songsters, well before daylight. From the hedgerow alongside the track leading to the cottage, a garden warbler is singing his heart out.

The last of the trees are now coming into leaf. The yellow-green fingered oak leaves have emerged, making the woods look as if they've been sprayed with mustard, and the ash buds are just opening. The soft green bracken croziers on the hillside are almost a foot tall. The sheep are moulting their thick coats, leaving lanolin-greasy tatters in the hedges and hooked on the barbed wire.

The pied flycatcher in the box on the terrace is still sitting on her seven sky-blue eggs. The male doesn't seem to feed her and she has to leave the nest to feed herself. As I'm watching them a rare humming bird hawkmoth lands on a clump of allysium and collects the nectar using its long proboscis. These beautiful moths are really bird-like. When I first saw one as a child I was convinced it was a humming bird, because of its size and the way it hovers over the flowers. Its long proboscis looks like a beak and its 'plumage' of furry, cinnamon-coloured hairs and its tail lend it an amazing similarity to a humming bird.

In the field a family group of siskins is plucking dandelion seeds. Their green plumage making them almost invisible in the dark green grass. They are ripping and tearing at the heads with undisguised relish, scattering the feathery seeds like children having a pillow fight.

26 MAY

The early morning brings heavy showers which clear later, leaving the afternoon sunny and hot. Rusty, the female kite, sits tight on her nest, wings spread out to shelter her offspring from the downpour. Not far from the nest a late lamb has been born in the shelter of an upturned tree root, maybe only minutes ago, and is still wet with mucous and unable to stand.

The resident male buzzard is perched in a large ash tree, close to the trunk and sheltered under its thick canopy of leaves. Through the dense curtains of rain, I can just make out the buzzard's strong head surrounding a caramel eye which betrays a soft flicker of light in it. Its dappled chocolate plumage merges with the dark shadow. Its yellow talons clutch the branch in vice-like grip. I know it's seen me, but it remains indifferent and aloof. It will need to keep its plumage dry if it wishes to fly later in the day and will sit there all morning until the rain stops or until it spots some movement in the field beneath, which may signify easy prey. If my neighbour lets her bantams out to roam in the field, one could easily become that prey. She loses her birds on a regular basis to buzzards or foxes, but this doesn't weaken her resolve to keep them.

Around midday the bluetit eggs in the box hatch and the parents begin their frenzied feeding schedule, bringing juicy grubs and caterpillars every couple of minutes, right up until nightfall. At the end of the two weeks the adults are emaciated and scraggy, their plumage becomes dulled as a result of the exhausting routine of feeding up to ten voracious youngsters. They ignore my presence near the box and refuse to be deflected from their feeding schedule, so strong is their instinct.

Unfortunately the long tailed tit's nest in the gorse scrub has been robbed despite its thorny protection. I surmise a magpie or jay is the culprit. The roof has been viciously ripped open and a trail of moss and white breast feathers is tell-tale evidence of the crime.

The 'oakwood' kite in the adjoining valley must now be sitting, as I see very little of the pair together, but today from the nesting wood, the female called gently to its mate as it circled above. Both kites later drifted languidly together over the valley in ever expanding circles and then glided low over the flock of sheep on the north west ridge. After about half an hour the female returned above the south west ridge and proceeded to fly down valley away from the nest. Silhouetted against the sky, she turned and flapped slowly back towards the wood, but now below the horizon, low over the bracken, so that her mottled plumage merged perfectly with the background. Without binoculars I would have lost her altogether. She flew past the nest, made several tight circles to ensure she was unobserved, then glided up into the nesting tree and disappeared from view. A little while after I heard her mewing again softly from the nest to her mate.

Kites are so different to peregrines. You are left in no doubt if you are caught entering a peregrine's territory - they scream at you and dive-bomb you, whereas a kite gives the impression that it is not nesting at all, that it just happens to be loitering around and will slip away and watch you from a distance, returning surreptitiously when you leave.

The pied flycatcher pair nesting in the box on the alder tree now have one pale blue egg, like a small oval of sky trapped in the dark interior. Their nest box is in a narrow gully formed by the stream, curtained by alder and hazel. On the lanes' verges the bluebells and stitchwort are faded to pastel shades and are being outshone by clusters of red campion and the deep lilac pendants of young foxgloves. Other banks are dominated by the blood-red umbels of valerian.

All day long the almost incessant singing of our resident willow and garden warbler tinkles from the large ash tree by the house.

27 MAY

I've seen merlins on a number of occasions in a valley, only a few miles inland, but have never been able to track them down properly and prove breeding. Because of their rarity and elusiveness they are one of the most difficult birds of prey to observe for longer periods. Usually the only reward is a quick glimpse of one as it skims low over the moor, and then melts into the vegetation and is lost. I decide to investigate an area where I'd seen birds in the previous year. It is not what I would call typical or even appropriate merlin country, but then I'm not a merlin!

It is a quiet, unfrequented valley because the small track into it peters out after a few miles at the treeline. There is a small stream running alongside a range of hills on one side and a dense spruce plantation on the other. I choose a bank at the side of the track to sit and wait. It gives me good views to the plantation and down over the valley. I haven't been sitting long before two sickle-shaped birds appear above the horizon of spruces, flying into the strong wind and virtually hovering side by side a few feet above the spikes of the trees, wondering, no doubt, whether I pose a significant danger. The smoky-blue male flies just behind the brown female. After hovering for about a minute they shear off and disappear. A little later while walking back along the ridge, I spot the nut brown female dashing along below me, following the course of a small stream, stopping several times to land on rocky outcrops and then darting onwards. I lose her in the distance. Merlins are like that. They keep to the high moors in spring and summer where they find a plentiful supply of pipits, whinchats and wheatears. But as they tend to fly fast and close to the ground, appearing and disappearing in seconds, they are easily missed. You are more likely to see them in winter when they move to the coast. In theory you can see them almost anywhere around here, but on most days you won't see them at all.

On my way back I pass a large upland pool where a colony of black headed gulls has found a home. Their whiteness seems out of place on this monotone green-ochre canvas of moorland. Some are sitting on their nests in reed clumps, others are swirling above, like pieces of paper lifted by the wind. Their raucous banter, too, violates the whispering spirit of the moorland wilderness.

31 MAY

I awake to a lambent sun caressing the still sleepy valley. From behind the trees' glittering tresses a garden warbler is serenading me with liquescent song.

The last three days have been balmy and temperatures have risen. Perhaps the summer is at last managing to impose its seasonal imperative. The valley finds itself in the throes of an infectious activity. A palpable urgency now governs bird behaviour - hunting and feeding become the defining activities. This makes the birds more visible. Like heated particles, they are in constant motion bringing food to their young. Today I allow myself to be captivated by the valley's magnetism and have little need or desire to venture farther afield.

The river, though, is still in flood from the earlier heavy rains. The little ringed plover has luckily chosen the highest point on the pebble bank for its nest scrape and it has survived the tearing waters. She sits alert on her eggs, but when a cawing crow swoops over the river, she flattens herself into the pebbles and becomes invisible. I observe her from a good distance so as not to disturb her. The chicks will be hatching in a day or so and if she is forced to leave her eggs at this juncture it could be fatal.

As I sit motionless on the riverbank, a female merganser

swims obliviously towards me with four fluffy ducklings in tow. She suddenly becomes aware of my presence and in an explosive panic rushes onwards, treading water and flailing with her wings. The youngsters paddle frantically behind, trying to keep up. They scuttle around the bend and tranquillity returns. Further along a pair of grey wagtails has built their nest on a small ledge, well camouflaged in the river bank. It contains four fully-feathered young. It is a joy to watch the parents hunting the insects which the warmth has now wheedled out in profusion and to admire the complex choreography as they pirouette and twist nimbly in the air catching their prey with precision.

The track to the house has a robin's nest with downy young, well concealed in the grassy bank and a chaffinch's nest cup of tightly woven moss in the hazel hedge has fully-grown nestlings.

The spring climaxes with a population boom and a period of warm summer days will be vital if these young birds are to survive and become parents themselves.

S U M M E R

Pied flycatcher pair

SUMMER

My childhood memories of summer are always associated with smells and sounds: the heavy sweet scent of hawthorn blossom or the sharp pungency of crushed bracken, the call of peewits and skylarks over the fields and the haunting cry of the curlew from the moors. They were, as I recall, long, languorous summer days where the atmosphere seemed to mesmerise every living thing. Of course, they are a compression of many summers, good and bad, where the bad is invariably repressed and the good lingers and becomes reinforced. Summers today in comparison seem less predictable, more erratic as far as the weather is concerned and certainly lack the profusion of animal and plant life I remember.

Spring always seems to arrive and disappear before one can fully grasp its presence and savour its burgeoning sensuality. Then summer is suddenly upon us in all its voluptuousness. Spring brings such promise with a new lease of life, and summer represents the culmination of it all, before rusting into autumn and introducing the chill of winter. It is at this late summer high-point that you particularly feel the delicate and precarious balance of the seasonal fulcrum. The delicate and translucent greens of late spring have darkened in the meantime, the foliage is now more luscious and heavy, creating deep, cool shadow and sharper outlines. It hangs heavy and limp, concealing all.

2 JUNE

The cuckoo is the bird probably most associated with summer in the public perception. Each year letter writers to the broadsheets compete to be the first to hear the returning bird's eponymous call notes. Each year the valley attracts a bird or two and its mellow, seductive call is heard throughout the summer months.

Over recent weeks I've often heard the cuckoo calling, usually in the early morning or late afternoon, from the hills behind the house, but I've only glimpsed him once, flying low over the bracken-covered hillside. He is quite difficult to spot even when calling, because his disembodied, bassoon-like notes carry long distances and he manages to produce a confusing ventriloquist effect. He has need to be secretive, because, like the other villains of the valleys, the hawks and owls, he is mercilessly mobbed by other smaller birds if discovered. It appears to be an irony of nature to make the cuckoo so similar in size and shape to a female sparrowhawk, although the two birds are absolutely unrelated. As if to offer the host birds a sporting chance of recognising them as a 'hawk-like' danger and thus deflecting their devious aims.

I am sitting in a small bright clearing of the plantation which covers one hillside, enjoying the glittering warmth after traipsing through the cold and sunless labyrinthine passages of the fir wood. I lean back against the bole of a fir tree, blissfully imbibing the quietude, when I see a smoky-grey bird appear from the depths of the plantation. It flies silently and swings up onto a branch of an oak tree about 50 metres away. It swiftly looks around, then drops into a clump of bracken from which it doesn't emerge. Then from within the same clump, there is a sudden staccato burst of angry notes. My curiosity aroused, I tiptoe across the glade to the bracken. As I reach the spot, the cuckoo flies off on silent wings, a diminutive russet ball of feathers in hot pursuit.

I peer into the bracken and discover the wren's nest, also built of bracken and thus superbly camouflaged, but this hasn't prevented the cuckoo finding it. In the roof of its domed abode is a large hole and through it I am able to glimpse several small wren's eggs and a large one, laid by the cuckoo. I've never witnessed a cuckoo attempting to use a wren as host before and my imagination is sorely taxed to visualise what will happen as the young cuckoo grows. I've seen several young cuckoos in pipits' nests and been amazed that the small, overworked pipits respond to these monstrously large fledglings squatting on their nests, their crimson gapes ever ajar for food. Individual cuckoos usually target specific host species, like pipits, reed warblers or dunnocks, but the wren is a very inappropriate host.

When I return to the spot several days later, I find the eggs cold and the nest deserted. I don't know for certain why this is, but can imagine the wren's trauma in discovering this vandal of a cuckoo attacking and damaging the nest was just too much.

4 JUNE

Each morning I wake expectantly, wondering how capricious

the weather will be. Any decision about where to go will be dependent on its early promise, and its moods will largely determine the birds I encounter.

Today begins auspiciously with a pale buzzard swooping low over the house and then circling effortlessly up into the blue. It takes no time at all for the morning sun to build up some strength and it coaxes the damp from the earth. Looking down from the ridge of the north-west hill, is like peering into a volcanic landscape with smoke emerging from the fissures between the valleys and clouds floating past below. The mist is soon dissipated, revealing the neat network of hedged, rhomboid fields which belies the often ramshackle state of the farms of which the fields are appurtenances. Only the nodules of these farmsteads, like knots in wool, interrupt the even pattern. The grass is bleached almost as white as the sheeps' bones on the moors and the sun burns deep into my bared skin as I recline on my bed of brittle sward. On ideal days like this summer memories from the past are rekindled, when I can imagine I am not in Wales at all, but in some southern European idyll.

By midday the buzzards and kites have found shady roosts in the densely foliaged oaks and sit there still as gargoyles, waiting for the cooler evening; blackbirds and thrushes rest on the ground, in the umbra of the shrubbery, beaks ajar, panting. Only the butterflies seem unaffected, fluttering animatedly from flower-head to flower-head. Sheep and cattle in the lower valley seek the shade of hedges and lambs crouch in the lee of peat hags and rocks on the hills. Even the buzzing midges seem lethargic, hanging in clouds beneath the limp foliage. The sun throbs in a clear sky, its rays shattering on the waxen leaves and siliceous grasses, shooting scintillas of light into the leaden heat. This mid-day period is the 'graveyard shift' for birds and bird-watchers alike. The light melts the shapes of familiar objects and sets them trembling in its hot convection, levitating the horizon into a shimmering mirage. A shroud of silence envelops the woods and valleys as songsters run out of breath and wing muscles become flaccid.

The frenetic activity of the late spring has now subsided and died away. The once turbulent rivers are reduced to a dribble. It seems only a few short weeks ago that the hedgerows and woods were filled with avian choristers and their nest-building activities. And only a short while before, the trees and hedges were just a tangle of seemingly lifeless twigs. The layers of green have now filled in the spaces, given shape to the bare scaffolding providing dense cover for the many young birds now having to fend largely for themselves.

5 JUNE

The hills have taken on the lightness of clouds, they are so pale and translucent, I feel they will be blown away with the early morning cloud. The sun silvers the farm roofs in the valley and they glisten through the milky mist below the pools which lie cast on the hills like fallen shards of sky.

The young bluetits - eight of them have survived to this stage - now have downy feathers and are looking healthy. Only a week ago they were more like larvae and appeared so vulnerable in their translucent pink-purply nakedness, their eyes still closed and their heads all gape, wobbling precariously on fragile, stringy necks. It is a miracle how rapidly they mutate from egg to fully fledged bird in barely a fortnight. The parents are flying into the box with small caterpillars every few minutes, desperate to satisfy their family's insatiable hunger. The buzzard is sitting tight on its eggs in the larch wood. It is now used to my presence and tolerates my passing quite close without flying off. All I can see when I look up into the tree is the bird's caramel-banded tail protruding beyond the mattress of sticks which forms its nest in the fork.

10 JUNE

Before midday, I climb up the slope behind the house to the beech copse and the lakes. The grass is still damp after the night's thunderstorm and slugs are everywhere slithering among the grass stems and even up the tree trunks.

The lake lies serene in the embrace of the hills and I saunter through the beech copse as if down a cathedral aisle. The great grey trunks soaring to the sky, holding the sheet of lake in their framework. On the far hill there is a dense flock of sheep. Below me, at the water's edge a heron is standing like Narcissus, seemingly transfixed by its own reflection in the water. In a flash it stabs, shattering the mirror, then withdraws its head with a large struggling trout impaled on its dagger-beak. It is an amusing sight, as it hesitates unsure of what to do next. It decides to wade back to the shore and then begins furiously shaking its head, but its beak has gone straight through the fish's torso and it refuses to come off. The heron shakes its head with increasing vigour until the fish is eventually dislodged and lands, still flopping, on the short grass. The bemused bird watches it for a few seconds before managing to get a vice-like grip on it, turn the trout's head earthwards and swallow it. The bulging shape slithers down inside the bird's stringy neck and it strops its beak clean on the grass. At this moment it catches sight of me and with a loud grunt, takes wing to the far side of the lake.

A kite is lifted effortlessly over the hill like a surfer on a wave, rising and falling on the swell. It then flies slowly along the brow before circling tightly to re-quarter the same area. Shortly it is joined by another three. They must belong to the two pairs which are breeding in the area.

The eggs of the pair nesting in the beech copse appear to have hatched, having escaped the predations of collectors and survived exposure to the heavy rains. Rusty is sitting in an elevated position on the nest, clearly sheltering her young beneath, but I'm unable to catch a glimpse of them. She remains frozen as I slink past about 200 metres away, the still dense beech foliage concealing and revealing her presence as the breeze sways its curtain back and forth in front of her. The sheep, always nervous of human presence, scatter before me, but one remains indifferently munching on the hillside. As I draw close, I notice that its eyes are misted and unseeing. It will find survival difficult for long on these treacherous hills without its sight, and will, no doubt, soon become carrion for the kites and ravens unless the farmer rescues it before this happens.

Back on the terrace, I soak up the warmth in the somnolent afternoon silence. Only the distant echoes of 'craaking' crows above the bubbling hiss of the stream and the clicking alarm call of a robin in the hedge penetrate the sound vacuum. Later a great spotted woodpecker chick-chicks from a large ash, and a grey squirrel comes onto the terrace, quite undisturbed by my presence and hops onto an old tree trunk, on which I've placed a sheep's skull. It holds the skull in its delicate paws and proceeds to gnaw at the dry bone, making loud grating noises, while flicking its tail nervously. Is it in need of calcium or is it using the skull to sharpen its teeth, I wonder?

With each day, the daylight hours lengthen irresistibly and even the sun seems reluctant to retire, but then it gutters and is gone, sunk into the deep velvet of the hills. A soft afterglow tinges the underbellies of the few remaining clouds, before that too dims into blackness.

15 JUNE

It's hazy but the warm sun is slowly dissipating the thin mist hanging in loose skirts around the hills. The pied flycatcher nesting on the terrace now has six young, almost a week old and covered with gossamer of grey down. I spend the morning watching the adults, like shuttles, flying back and forth in quick succession with food. The young bluetits in the box behind the house departed the nest two weeks ago, leaving behind one addled egg.

June is the apogee of the flowering plant world. Blossom is bursting open everywhere - on the hedgerows, in the fields, on the moors and on the coastal cliffs. The ochre hills are suffused with a soft green as the new bracken spreads its fronds over the old. The meadows are pointillist canvases of buttercups and brick-red sorrel, or sidereal firmaments of daisies. The insect kingdom flourishes in parallel with the profusion of blossom: dragon- and damselflies dart erratically around the ponds and marshy areas, bees suck meticulously from each bloom and butterflies, spoilt for choice, flutter back and forth indecisively

- skippers, painted ladies, meadow blues and tortoiseshells.

The full-rigged oaks and ashes soften the hard edges of walls and fences, curtaining off the avian theatre playing within, releasing only the voices, which have also reached a culmination of intensity and variety. From the one big ash next to the cottage on one early evening I hear pigeons cooing gently, a blackbird fluting, the melodic phrases of garden warbler and the melancholic song of willow warbler as well as pied flycatcher calling. From the cloistered passages of the beeches wood warblers practice their descending evensong scales. In the soft early evening light it resembles a gothic chapel: the tall grey trunks towering to the vaulted canopy. Sunlight filtering through the trees' translucent coppery leaves feigning stained glass windows and scattering mosaics of gold on the cool woodland floor. In the depths of the plantation jays are chattering and from its margins chiffchaffs are calling.

21 JUNE

Desperate for fresh air and exercise, after the last few days cooped in by the weather, I decide to brave the elements and battle around a large upland lake only a few miles inland, despite the persistence of the driving rain. It is impossible to hear anything above the rain's timpani and no bird is flying of its own volition. I slog around the water-logged fringe of the lake, not expecting to see a thing, but am pleasantly surprised when a faint fluting note is carried to me across the water - unmistakably the call of a common sandpiper. A quarter of a mile further round and the bird flies up, gliding low over the lake to join its mate. I don't think they have eggs or young, as they exhibit no alarm at my presence. Normally at this time of year they would have young or a late clutch, but the extremely inclement weather may have frustrated their attempts. Any large upland lake hereabouts boasts at least one pair of sandpipers - often the only birds breeding on them. From the soaking grass, deep purply-red heads of lousewort are emerging into the light and the minute flower-stars of bedstraw nestle between the nibbled stalks.

The moor is revived by the sun. On its steeper slopes where it is matted thickly with bracken, heather, bilberry and coarse grass it resounds only to the irregular bleat of lost lambs. Even now it only reveals its bird and insect life when I walk over it, flushing pipits like fleas from it's hairy pelt, wheatears from the scree, and moths and flies from their tangled refuges.

The respite in the weather has also persuaded others to venture abroad and as I return to the valley walking below the lead mine a tinkle of dislodged shale reverberates off the hills as a small band of climbers, utilising the dry spell, make their way upwards above the old workings.

Back in the lower valley, I am amazed at the contrast to the bleakness of the moors. The lanes' verges are a riot of colour, offering rich bouquets of flowers to the wanderer: delicate, light-headed harebells nod alongside the bright yellow hawkbit and the dusty-blue scabious, clumps of deep purple bell heather clash with lighter pinky-purple rosebay willow herb; and above these, twists of apricot and pink honeysuckle are woven into the hedges. The woods are a wall of dense blanketing green. On those few slopes spared the incessant gnawing of sheep, plum-dark bilberries glisten from among rusty leaves and, unexpectedly, in places, small groups of saffron and olive boletus peak through the wiry grass. I need to be early, though, if I wish to pick enough for a meal, because in the damp evenings the slugs devour them with great appetite.

Sometimes the sky mimics the landscape, fabricating layers of cloud hills beyond the real horizon, so that I have the impression the land goes on for ever. Where the cloud is torn, patches of cerulean show through. The keen light brings everything into sharp focus, etching keen-edged outlines around the rocks and trees. Only in the far distance do the shapes become smudged and softened by the haze. By late afternoon the valley appears completely devoid of animal life. Before the light goes I decide to see how the other kite pair is progressing in the adjoining valley.

Kites, very visible during most of the year, almost vanish during the breeding season. Their ability to 'disappear' is a behavioural trick the kite must have learned during the period of acute persecution - it could not have survived otherwise. It is difficult to imagine when you watch these large birds flapping leisurely over the hills clearly silhouetted against the sky, that they could ever be difficult to see. But when the females are sitting on eggs or young the males are exceedingly circumspect in their behaviour near the nest, so I hadn't been unduly surprised not to have seen a kite over the oakwood in this valley for some time. But today I'm more than ever convinced that something is wrong - the nest has definitely been robbed. There is again no sign of either bird, so I feel I can afford to approach the site and examine the nest more closely. The steep, bracken-covered slope behind the wood allows me to climb above the nest and peer right into it below. A large pile of sticks has been wedged in the fork of a medium-sized oak and lined with clumps of fleece and pink binding string. As I feared, there are no eggs or young in the shallow cup. To witness this failure leaves me with a profound sense of loss and emptiness. It will remain a mystery why and how the nest has been robbed - was it a corvid opportunist, taking the eggs while the kite was momentarily off the nest (kites are not normally that careless) or was it egg collectors? I will never know. I can only hope that the pair will return to try again next year.

24 JUNE

As the weather has considerably improved, I decide to venture onto the high moor to see if I can locate the elusive dunlin. Only very few of these diminutive waders nest in mid-Wales and trying to find them is like searching for the proverbial needle in a haystack. Of course, they are well-nigh impossible to locate visually - 15 or so thrush-sized birds hiding somewhere in up to 100 square miles of moorland! The best way to find them is to listen for their characteristic little song in the Spring. However the days on the high moor when there is no wind can be counted on one hand and the wind has the infuriating habit of snatching away even the most vocal of sounds, despite the fact that you may be close to their source. And this is one of those windy days.

One area where they are known to breed is only a few miles from my valley. It is a daunting moorland expanse, dotted with small pools and peat bogs.

I leave the mountain road and cut inland, climbing slowly to the upland moor. There are no paths and it is hard going through the coarse tussock grass, over rocks and through marshland. It seems to never end, my legs become more leaden as the morning wears on. Care has to be taken to avoid a broken ankle or sinking up to my thighs in bog. Keeping an eye on the vegetation is essential. They are the indicators of safe or unsafe terrain. I am forced to take wide circles around cotton grass or thick reed, where I know it will be very wet and treacherous underfoot. As I stumble onwards, I think it can't be any more arduous trying to cross the Siberian tundra.

I scan the treeless horizon for signs of life. What was only a few weeks ago an empty expanse, is now alive with pipits that start up at my feet every few metres and seep-seep in alarm. Skylarks, too, rise and shower their song into the ear of the sky. Several upland pools lie scattered as if fortuitously on the blanket of the gently undulating moorland, the soft shadows in its folds lending a sketchy shape to its flatness. It is here among these pools and the peat bogs that the dunlin are to be found.

Despite traipsing for miles through the knee-high rush, across gushing streams and wading through peat pools for hours, I catch not even a whiff of a dunlin. At one point, though, I do convince myself that I hear a snatch of song but no sight of a bird to prove it. On these open moors, where the wind and your own heartbeat are often the only audible sounds, it is easy to fantasise and imagine hearing other sounds. I do in fact hear, however, and see a lovely male golden plover guarding its territory from a hillock of heather. He stands stiff and upright in his golden chain mail and black breastplate, like some miniature knight prepared to defend his bailey. He keeps me under observation until I am well outside his territory. Close by, I inadvertently send a pair of red grouse whirring down the hillside. They are also an endangered species, as the sheep devour more and more of the heather uplands. Among some lichen-spattered rocks I almost tread on two small lizards, tempted out by the sunnier weather, but still quite lethargic, lying there quite still like discarded shoe laces.

Despite being gloriously sunny, with scarce a wisp of cloud in the sky, the wind is forceful and keeps the smaller birds, like meadow pipits and wheatears, on the ground unless disturbed. The only birds on the wing seem to be the raptors. Several buzzards are curious about my presence in these usually deserted moors, a kite patrols in the distance and a single peregrine streaks overhead towards its eyrie in the valley.

In the evening I take a short stroll up the lane behind the cottage. Rhododendrons, which flourish on the acidic soil here lend a Chinese water colour quality to the woodland fringe behind old Evans's barn. Pale mauve silken blossoms float diaphanously on deep pools of sylvan shadow. While admiring the blooms, my eye is caught by a redstart carrying succulent grubs to its newly-hatched brood in the eaves of the disused barn, utilising the last moments of the rapidly fading light. As it lands, it flashes its tail - the deep, reddish colour of stripped cork-oak. The swallows, too, are flicking in and out of the barn through the gap above the doors, taking food to their hungry chicks in the eaves. All birds with growing youngsters at this time of the year have to make full use of every minute of daylight to ensure their survival.

As the young birds fledge and depart their nests, their parents cease singing. Their sexual and territorial urges are assuaged and they are now fully occupied with feeding their ravenous broods. The frenetic energies which characterised the spring and early summer are burned up and the lethargy born of fulfilment ushers in a slow winding down period.

Despite the lengthening shadows, seeping like dark water from the woodland edges, old Snowyhead, the male kite is refusing to retire for the night and is slowly quartering the brow of the ridge above the cottage, in the hope of discovering a last meal before the light is snuffed. I watch his dark silhouette as it oscilates, like a sleek moth on the shoulder of the hill before it too is drowned by the shadow.

26 JUNE

Although the morning begins cool and cloudy, as so often here, the afternoon brings dramatic change. The clouds flee and the valley is flooded with light and warmth. There is an atmosphere of calm serenity. Sheep are bleating softly from the grassy slopes, a buzzard is gently mewing from on high and a ragged streamer of jackdaws comes laughing over the ridge.

Of those peregrine eyries that have survived, all have full grown eyasses now. In the 'Scottish Glen' (I call it this because it reminds me of a valley in the West Highlands) the eyrie contains three. It must be a very good year for prey, because it is not common for more than two fledglings to survive to maturity. I am thrilled to see that this pair has been successful, because the eyrie had been abandoned for the last two years after being robbed by egg collectors.

To begin with there is no sign of the adults, but the young birds are clearly aware of my presence across the gulch and watch me warily, in between vigorous flapping exercises with their wings. While I'm watching, the tiercel suddenly sweeps in with prey in his talons, landing on the narrow ledge alongside the young. I can't identify its prey, but it could be a song- or mistle thrush. It proceeds to tear at the carcass and gently offers fragments to the hungry eyasses. I think the fact that this pair seems to have learned the virtues of silence - at least when I've been near the eyrie they haven't been vocal -

may have saved them. The young birds are beautiful: their heads dark, bleeding into the moustachial stripe, their breasts a rich cream and their backs a peaty-slate colour.

As I walk back through the village, I'm forced into the hedge by a flock of sheep being driven down the lane. Like a flood wave of fleecy foam it surges past. The dogs with their sharp intelligence and alertness keep them compact, snapping at wayward stragglers until they've all passed in a cloud of dust. In trampling the verges they have disturbed insects which are caught by swallows jinking down the lane behind them. These are joined by house martins, flinging themselves over the hedge like a flight of arrowheads, glinting steely-blue or white as they twist in the light and zoom up to their nest cups under the overhanging gable ends of the Forestry Commission houses.

  In the evening I clear the pied flycatcher's old nest from the box on the terrace in preparation for Winter roosting tits and, hopefully, the flycatchers' return next year. The nest had been built of dry grass, interwoven with strands of moss and adorned with several dry ivy and oak leaves. One porcelain blue infertile egg remains in the cup.

28 JUNE

In the night, spectral calls from the resident pair of tawny owls puncture the silence – sharp thwick, thwick, thwick notes ricocheting back and forth. One is sitting in the spruce next to the house and as I lie awake staring up at the night sky through the roof light, I see its dark silhouette ghost across the pane.

The morning is ushered in by a strong westerly bringing showery clouds over the cusp of the hills. The birds have been silenced by the strong winds and cool weather - such a contrast with the previous month. The pied flycatchers appear to have vanished into thin air, they are neither heard nor seen. I find already that I miss their pied flickering in the canopies and their chirpy song.

In the early morning, from my window, I see Snowyhead flying down the valley, followed by Rusty, his mate. Their young must be quite large now and the parents feel it is safe to leave them alone for a while. They fly past a buzzard which, I'm sure is actually 'enjoying' the strong wind. It circles, its head is extended and its beak opens and closes as it mews with vigour. Then it plunges and takes a long glide as if savouring the joys of the uplift.

I feel it should now be safe for me to visit the kites' nest at the head of the valley, as the young must almost be ready for their first independent flight. I try to sneak up to the site by hugging the edge of the plantation where my human form is camouflaged against its dark background. I then keep below the ridge of the hill, out of sight, only emerging at the summit where I have a clear view over the surrounding area. I am still far enough away to avoid disturbing the birds and can observe them from an elevated position. Snowyhead appears and flies over me, looking down with his keen eyes, assessing the danger. He gives no appearance of being agitated or alarmed, and disappears as quickly as he's come. I scan the beech trees through binoculars. They are still full-leafed, but I am soon able to locate the fork in which the large nest of sticks has been built. I can see clearly the chestnut back of Rusty, her plumage marked with fine black striations, giving her the appearance of being composed of sticks herself. She must sense my presence, because she raises her pale head and turns it slowly to watch me, her sharp beak clearly silhouetted against the sky. She looks so regal on her arboreal throne, surveying her domain, her rich, feathered robe flowing around her. I don't glimpse the chicks but am relieved to know that they are there. Not wishing to outstay my welcome or cause her to fly off, I wander away towards the lake. The sun, which is now quite hot again, is teasing the moisture from the earth and the lake's surface is covered in a steamy cloud. I can just make out a male tufted duck, like a ghost galleon, floating in and out of the wreathing mist. In the wet grassland around the lake's margins, silky lilac pyramids of common spotted orchid blossoms peek out from the whorls of browned grass. The warmth appears to have freed the silenced voices for a last fanfare of notes. A male whinchat bursts into song from his perch on an old willow log lying in the bracken. A female redstart, alarmed at my presence, 'tut-tuts' me from a large beech and several chiffchaffs repeat their onomatopoeic songs from the willow scrub.

Towards evening silence once again reigns. In the valley bottom, the farmer is mowing his pastures and, although this is Sunday, he continues working into the twilight, the dull drone of his tractor being almost the only sound coming from the throat of the valley.

10 JULY

So many days this year haven't lived up to the summer day idyll, and today is another of them. Enormous cumulus clouds race across the sky like a herd of pale elephants. Patches of blue are revealed fleetingly, then occluded. The wind tears at the dense foliage of the trees and the paths are littered with broken twigs and bunches of leaves; the tall firs creak and groan as they resist the wind's force. Not the sort of day you expect in mid-summer, but nevertheless dry and good for an invigorating walk along the foot of the valley, where the hills provide a barrier to the wind's violence.

The river which flows through the lower valley passing several small villages, offers an enjoyable and easy walk. A narrow, Hansel and Gretel path hugs the bank. Not many years ago, before Lord Beeching's butchery, it carried a section of the West Coast railway. Now its hardcore base is overgrown with thick grass, tall nettles and plantain. Only a few rotted sleepers and sections of rusting track betray its orignal purpose. Dense hawthorns, alders and willow overarch the walk, their interlocking fingers caging a rich collection of small songsters. The rythmic rattle of metal wheels and asthmatic wheezing of steam engines has given way to the aurally more pleasing jingling of garden warblers and chirping of goldfinches.

The river is shallow and broader along this stretch, flowing rapidly over its pebbly bed. The sun reflected from the water's ripples projects rhythmic waves of light in the branches of the bordering willows. It is beloved of wagtails, both pied and grey, because it offers a rich menu of insects. The dipper, too, is partial to the shallow, fast-sweeping waters where it can jump into the flow and wheedle its food from beneath the pebbles without too much effort. Today I am also lucky to catch a glimpse of a kingfisher, hunched up beneath the swaying fronds of a weeping willow, the usual vibrant colour of its plumage drained by the shade. It is so intent on watching the water for the tell-tale shadows of fish, that it doesn't notice my approach on the path above it.

The lanes and hedgerows offer a rich harvest of berries at this time of the year, both strawberries and blackberries, but it is often a battle to beat the slugs and the birds. Along a damp lane which leads away from the river wild strawberries, like

Goshawk at nest

small drops of blood lie among the tangle of runners on a steep grassy bank. It takes me less than an hour of diligent picking to amass enough for a tasty dessert.

The lane continues up onto the hilltop which overlooks the wide valley. The dense growth of young bracken beneath the woodland exudes its typically sweet-acrid aroma as I wade through it, bruising the young stems. Where the trees had been cleared two years ago, there is, from this distance, what appears to be a large purple silk scarf draped on the hillside, but on approaching, it turns into a rectangle of densely growing foxgloves. They are rapid colonisers of cleared land. Lower down, the larches are adorned with this year's small, bright green cones, exuding tears of resin. A family of long-tailed tits careers through the trailing branches, chattering animatedly, before flying off to the next tree. A willow tit, the characteristic pale bar on its primaries clearly visible, emerges for a moment from the tangle of needles, then disappears into the canopy again. High above, a pair of ravens are playing aerial games, gambolling and diving like high-spirited children.

By the end of my walk, I am able to tot up forty different species of birds that I've seen in only a couple of hours, not a bad tally at this time of year and in such a short time.

In the late afternoon, from the valley fields there is a constant symphony of bleating as the sheep are brought down off the moors for shearing. On a normal day it would be warm and sunny, but today is not a good one for the sheep to lose their thick and protective coats. Old Hywel Evans, who keeps his flock on the hills above the lead mine, is watching his dogs bring them down. They weave in and out and around the stragglers, carefully funneling them down to the paddock. He and his sheep will be very distressed if the weather doesn't quickly turn for the better.

He leans on the gate shouting instructions to his dogs through his ill-fitting and stained dentures. They clatter around in his mouth like ice cubes in a glass of whisky. His greasy old mac is tied at the waist with fencing string and his gnarled, stubbly face is tanned by the wind. I'm never sure whether he is really as poor as he looks or whether his money is stuffed under the mattress, but with prices for sheep falling all the time, the smaller hill farmers certainly don't have it feather-bedded.

16 JULY

It is late morning and before I leave the house the rain starts. Thick fluvial braids unravel from the sky and sweep in rippling skeins across the hills, driving all animal life cowering into sheltering crevices. Heavy drops are beating down on the foliage, the trees shudder under the weight, but then it abates almost as soon as it begins. I take my chance and drive down to the sea.

The strong Westerlies have blown groups of shearwaters close to the shore. They are birds you don't see easily, or if you do they are invariably far out to sea, appearing the size of midges. Today I can follow their stiff-winged flight from close quarters as they hug the contours of the waves, turning alternatively to reveal their white underbellies and dark chocolate backs. There are a few snow-white gannets too, bombing into the water, then emerging with a shudder from the cloying liquid into the air again, before continuing their circling on the look-out for fish near the surface.

The air is saturated with abrasive sea salt that claws at my skin. The cliff ledges are blushing with flowering crusts of stonecrop and pink cushions of thrift border the edges. Thick, fleshy leaves of navelwort fountain from the crevices and the wind wafts the sweet fragrance of burnet roses to titillate my nose as I force my way through its thorny tangles. It is too cold to sit and watch for long and I leave these thalassic birds to their element.

23 JULY

The day starts disconcertingly, with small frogs being flushed out of the cold water tap. The water supply comes from a spring on the hill behind the house and it is sealed by a concrete lid. I can only assume the frogs gain entry by climbing up the long grass stems and into the overflow pipe. They obviously spawn there and leave by the same route. Around the pools and lakes at this time of the year the grass is often alive with such tiny frogs, only recently emerged from their aquatic domain. Herons are quick to avail themselves of such an easy meal without having to undergo the usual patient waiting for fish. In the field below the spring, I can see two of them stalking stiffly through the long grass like tall and slender ballet dancers, stabbing every so often into the ground.

This hasn't been a good year at all. Despite the promise of a warm and dry spring and summer, it has been cool and wet - catastrophic for ground-nesting birds and fledglings. Today is no different, beginning with light showers broken by the odd sunny spell. I utilise the longer breaks to weed the rockery of some of the more rampant of the wild plants: rosebay willow herb, dandelion and herb robert, buttercups and nettles, but leave the vetch, bilberry, teasel and, of course, the wild strawberries. Weeding is easy on this soil, because it is finely crumbled rock, like a coarse sand and the roots come away easily. Among the rosebay I discover a fat elephant hawk moth caterpillar with its large painted 'eyes' to frighten-off predators.

Late afternoon, during a lull, I stroll up the valley road, past the old lead mine. The ruins of the roofless winding house with its crumbling walls looks like a smashed skull, with ferns growing from its window-orifices. On the hill behind it, sheep are ascending slowly in single file like humble pilgrims departing a shrine. One of the fields close by has the appearance of a green firmament, speckled with white stars, which on closer inspection turn out to be fresh horse mushrooms. They provide a wonderful side-dish for dinner that evening, after I discard the few riddled with grubs.

Both the following days and nights bring continuous heavy showers and strong blustery winds; the sky lies on the hills like armour plate - heavy and oppressive. It is such a pity that the weather is so obstinate because the hills are looking their best now, with a light purple dusting of heather, interspersed with freckles of chrome-yellow gorse and a touch here and there of pastel blue harebells and mauve of betony. There is a good crop of bilberries this year and, despite the rain, I manage to fill two sandwich boxes in under an hour from one small patch above the fir line.

I don waterproofs and climb the north-eastern ridge. The stream is as full as in winter and rushes in torrents down the valley; the ground is as leaky as a colander and water trickles out of every pore and crevice. I climb up through the hanging oakwood which extends up from the road and then through the bracken, following the sheep tracks, slipping and sliding as I try to maintain my foothold. Three buzzards are circling above me, one of them mewing. They are probably hungry and are utilising a lull in the weather to take wing again. A female kestrel hovers below me, with what looks like a jess dangling from its leg.

Over the lakes a lone kite is circling, while a little below on the hillside leading to the lakes two men are inserting fence posts. Their hammering reverberates around the valley like a loud expletive in a gentlemen's club. The fencing, too, in its strict geometry of containing lines offends against nature's anarchy. The farmer has cleared the whole hillside of its rich gorse and bracken scrub and reseeded it with fescue grass and root crop for the sheep.

Four ravens plunge over the brow of the hill, croaking with annoyance at the intruding figures. A pair of mistle thrushes feed readily on the freshly planted ground and a female wheatear rummages among an overlooked clump of large thistles on one of which a painted lady butterfly is languidly flapping. As I pass the oak wood by the cottage I'm surprised to hear a wood warbler trilling, but the song is snapped off like a twig before completion, as if the bird realises it's pointless now. The sky is now clear and the western horizon tugs at a sun reluctant to vacate the cloying blue.

28 JULY

The beach adjacent to the town is almost deserted. Scribbles of seaweed mark the tideline. Most holiday-makers have departed in despair at the inclement weather. One or two hardy families remain stubbornly determined to ignore the weather's efforts to drive them away. At sea small numbers of sandwich terns are fishing. They buoyantly quarter the shallower waters flying back and forth on sharp wings, scrutinising the surface for smaller fish. Further out, into the deeper waters, gannets are plunging, closing their scissor wings and falling, one after the other, like a hail of missiles into the sea, sending plumes of water upwards. They have clearly located a shoal of fish and are diving in frenzied raids. They emerge, rest on the water for a few seconds before lumbering back into the air to dive again. Unlike the terns which arise with their catch held firmly in their beaks, I've never seen a gannet with a fish - they swallow them under water, perhaps to avoid attacks by pirate gulls. The shore itself has almost as few birds as people. The usual desultory groups of black-headed and herring gulls are preening and bathing at the tide's edge, together with a single pair of curlews, several ringed plovers, and dunlin. On the sand two oystercatchers are squabbling over a cockle. Large blobs of jelly fish and crab carapaces lie scattered on the sand, cast up by the recent violence of the sea.

At last the weather appears to be changing for the better. Despite a light shower in the morning, the day becomes bright and sunny. There is a pregnant mystery in the hills, an expectancy of things about to happen. I decide to follow the brighter weather as it captures the mountains, driving out the sullen cloud. A mountain walk will provide good exercise if not some interesting bird life.

From the foot of the 700 meter peak I decide to tackle, the crags scowl down at me like angry gods. I clamber gently up the slope which is clothed in purple heather and bilberry, until the bare visages of the rocks rise menacingly above me. But the climb is well worth it: I'm presented with a wide panorama of camel-humped hills and the distant haze of the sea and broad, meandering estuary. Only a few long cylindrical clouds lie still on the pale blue sky like beached whales.

Just below me is a small, secluded pond which wasn't visible as I climbed up. It is fringed with rushes and starred with water lilies in full flower. Its pristine surface, though, is suddenly corrugated by movement. With binoculars I'm able to pick out a small bird which slides under the water again almost as soon as it surfaces. The rusty neck, neat, spheroid, tail-less body and the whitish patch near the lower mandible reveal it to be a little grebe feeding a brood of chicks, half hidden in the sedge. It is quite unusual to find these birds at such an altitude and on what are usually lifeless pools.

The sun is warm and, lying in my pliable bed of heather, plucking bilberries, as I watch the family antics of the grebes, I have no desire to descend again to the shadowed valley. But the golden glow in the sky and the pink-tinged clouds warn me that the day is slowly seeping away.

2 AUGUST

Although much of the coast here is flat, there are one or two sections of cliff, which offer ideal opportunities for observing littoral life and seabirds in their element.

The sky is blue and the sun is shining, but it is only feigning summer - the cutting wind makes my eyes water. The cliff-top view is exhilarating; white horses dance on the waves and the sea is a heaving broth of checkered grey and greenish-blue as the shadows of the scudding clouds mottle its surface. The cliff top is a matted growth of blackthorn and gorse, friseured and sculpted asymmetrically by the prevailing winds. The narrow track meanders through it, sometimes dangerously close to the crumbling cliff face.

Below me, in the sea three seals poke their wet, bewhiskered snouts above the waterline and sniff the air, before rolling back into the depths. Another lies sun-bathing on a flat rock which is also adorned with four statuesque cormorants, drying their wings, like black griffins. The usual gulls – black-headed, herring and great black-backs are wheeling and screaming, on the lookout for easy pickings. A Manx shearwater on its board-like wings skims the breakers way out to sea. Closer to the cliffs two or three fulmars circle effortlessly around the cliff face. The rock ledges, only a month ago chock-a-block with razorbills and guillemots, are now empty. Only the white splashes of guano are a reminder of their recent presence.

I count four pairs of stonechats during my short cliff walk and one of them has three fully-fledged, darkly speckled youngsters in tow. These stonechats look very much like young robins and without the give-away presence of the adults could easily be confused. They sit atop the gorse or blackthorn like miniature sentries, so unlike the several whitethroats I spot, which dive for cover as soon as I approach and churr their annoyance from undergrowth hideaways. Rock pipits forage beneath the scrub on the steeper sections of the cliffs.

The path eventually brings me down to sea level again and to a small bay with a small pebbly beach backed by a grassy carpet interwoven with thrift and sea aster. There, standing immobile and almost invisible against the pebbles, is a pair of ringed plovers. They are one of our daintiest and prettiest breeding wader, with their pastel-tawny backs, black breast crescent and orange-rimmed eyes. It is an ideal nesting spot for them here, but they have become quite a rare breeding bird along this stretch of coast in recent years and it could be that they are just visiting. They do appear to be indifferent to my sudden appearance and show no sign of nervosity which I would expect if they were breeding.

The regular presence of visitors, many with unleashed dogs, has created disturbance in their traditional territories and resulted in a sharp decline in the ringed plovers' breeding success.

The blackthorn scrub, which offered refuge to many a summer songster, is now virtually silent. Only when I wander through a small cliff-top wood, owned by the National Trust, do I hear a few, tentative notes from a pair of coal tits and a solitary chiffchaff.

I return to the valley late in the afternoon, but immediately miss the movement and sounds of the coast. In spring the valley is bubbling with activity and bird song reverberates from every bush and tree, but now it is taciturn.

4 AUGUST

Two young buzzards are mewling like abandoned babies from a group of large larches on the hill, as their parents circle, looking for food. A brood of spotted flycatchers is flitting back and forth from the low branches of an ash tree, chasing the late midges and flies. These birds are not as common here as the pied flycatcher and, unless seen chasing insects, can be easily missed because their dull plumage and retiring behaviour are excellent camouflage. I enjoy watching the young birds learning hunting skills. In early August the fully fledged offspring of our nesting birds can be encountered everywhere.

The moors are alive with pipits, which start up regularly from the tussocks as you walk, and tseep-tseep their alarm into the wind. Wheatears dart about among the stone-strewn hillsides and stubby-tailed swallows begin to gather in twittering parties on the telegraph wires, preparing for their departures. The firs are alive with young tits of various species chasing after each other in the canopy. In and out of some gorse bushes close by, a family party of great tits is playing 'follow-the-leader', cheeping animatedly to maintain contact. It is difficult to imagine that the young birds' dull, brassy plumage will shortly transmute into the glossy black, white and lemon of the adults.

From the upper valley, the recently mown field below looks like green corduroy. A ragged party of black-headed gulls has invaded it to scavenge for the invertebrates exposed in the stubble. Their raucous shrieks carry far up into the valley. At this time of the year, most of the pasture fields are close-shaven, as if by a hairdresser, in clean patterned lines. Hay is rolled into giant Swiss-roll sculptures and left in the fields to dry. The song birds have gone mute and, apart from the distant gulls, the only sounds are the deep rustle of leaves in the warm breeze and the groaning of leaf-laden limbs against the background gurgle of the stream.

The fir wood behind the house has now almost been cleared by the Forestry Commission tree-fellers. Neat piles of severed trunks lie beside the track. The pungent scent of resin from their bleeding wounds pervades the evening air. Most of the birds that nested here in former years have disappeared. Two or three hardy tree pipits have filled the void, utilising the few trees left standing as singing posts from which to launch their parachuting display glides. Deep scars have been left in the ground by the tractors pulling the felled trees off the slopes. These will be filled later by rain and provide ideal habitats for frogs to lay their spawn and mosquitoes to breed as well as sources of drinking water for mammals and birds.

On a still summer afternoon like this one, when not a sound is to be heard and nothing stirs, it is as if deadly rays have eradicated all life and the valley becomes a strange place. There is not even the plaintive bleat of a distant lamb, nor a winged creature in the incandescent sky - I feel as if I'm the only one left alive, and the valley has become a green-lined tomb waiting to inter the last expiring being.

10 AUGUST

As I'm making my way through the sand dunes, weaving between the coarse tufts of marram grass, I'm surprised by the high-pitched alarm call from a bird somewhere ahead of me. For a few moments I can't identify the source of the cries, but know it must be a wader of some sort. Then I spot it as it begins to flutter some metres away to my left, dragging its wing on the ground as if it were broken. I walk towards it, as it continues calling with appealing insistence. As I draw close, the ringed plover's wing is suddenly 'healed' and the bird flies up with no difficulty, to land on the summit of a sand dune, from where it continues to mewl at me.

I retrace my steps and search the ground and then discover them – two salt and pepper coloured, fluffy chicks lying pressed to the ground, playing possum until given permission to move by their parents. Their camouflage is perfect among the moss and lichen on the pebbly ground. They are endearing creatures with their large eyes, shining like dark chestnuts, their finely tapered bills, long gawky legs tucked under them and fine downy plumage. I walk quickly away before an inquisitive herring gull or crow appears on the horizon. They would see these chicks simply as dainty morsels, providing a quick calorie fix. I am doubly pleased to find that at least one pair of plovers has been successful, because with all the disturbance these dunes and beaches are subjected to during the summer, it is a virtual miracle for these young to have fledged.

19 AUGUST

The late summer sun still has considerable strength. The grass on the poor gravely soil here is soon parched to straw. In the

Young Great Tits

field behind the cottage a few late chrome-yellow umbels of ragwort blaze like beacons, attracting a dense menagerie of insects to their luminescent blossoms.

The bog, as always from a distance, appears deserted. The air is brittle and still. I wander languidly along the old railway track not expecting to see much sign of life in this heat, but then nature conspires to confound my preconceptions. In one small hawthorn shrub on the edge of the bog I see simultaneously a young male and a female redstart, a blue tit still with its baby yellow mandibles, a scolding sedge and diffident willow warbler and two young whinchats perched on top and then, as if to complete this tableau, a grey squirrel scuttles up the trunk to join them. It is like a fantasy picture in a children's nature book! As I draw close they scatter and disappear in the immensity of the bog.

In a thick bed of phragmites a few remaining reed warblers are chuntering, hidden from view by the dense lattice of dry stems. This is a good time to see young birds of many of our breeding species. Where the adults are secretive and cautious, the young are inexperienced and readily expose themselves naively to prying eyes of both friend and foe.

On my return journey I stop by a small river. At this point it flows in a straight line and is like a scintilla of fallen sky, transporting its clouds on the slow ebbing current to the sea, its muddy banks glistening in the late afternoon sun. As soon as I climb up onto the bank, exposing myself against the sky, I hear the unmistakable three-note kyoo, kyoo, kyoo of a greenshank. As I walk towards the sound, seven birds fly up, on slender wings, their dark charcoal backs divided by white slashes, clearly visible as they fly low down river. These birds will have come from Scotland on their migratory route south. Further down, six young goosanders, like children at the seaside are chasing each other through the shallows, ducking and diving with palpable enjoyment.

22 AUGUST

The sky is bubbling with cloud. Although it is hot, the air has a freshness which makes the heat bearable. There is a purple blush of heather through the olive foliage and mosaics of light shimmer on the peat-dyed pools. From the heather-covered slopes a honeyed fragrance is wafted down the valley. In birch scrub at the edge of the plantation a twittering of redpolls is audible and, as I pass, the small flock shoots into the sky like a burst of grapeshot and disappears over the fir line.

The narrow mountain road is aflutter with family groups of pipits and wagtails. Wheatears are still on the hills building up reserves for the migratory journey and all the hirundine species are still to be seen around the lakes, chittering in small flocks. Bees and wasps are hovering over the few late-flowering plants and, on the terrace, a peacock butterfly attempts to draw nectar from the pink flowers on the deck-chair canvas.

26 AUGUST

Yet another balmy day with a clear blue sky and only a few tatters of cloud teased by a slight breeze. Despite the warm sun, though, there is now a presience of autumn in the air. It is an ideal day for a mountain walk.

I take an easy route along a narrow lane that meanders slowly upwards through airy oakwoods to fizzle out where it emerges onto the bare moor. The old stone walls are bearded with moss and the tree roots clutch at the verges like wizened fingers. The crowns of the hills are purpled with heather. The rowans and hawthorns are laden with berries. The bracken on the lower slopes is already tinged with rust at the edges, although the trees are still green and full-leaved.

The breeding season is once again over and everywhere passerines are avidly feeding on perhaps the last explosion of insect life before the autumn. On a cliffy outcrop an old raven's nest is wedged in a ledge, a few sooty feathers still clinging to the sticks. The rocks around it are decorated with tufts of flowering heather and gorse. This nest will no doubt be reused next year. In a wet dell, a family of whinchats, the young now fully grown, are chasing crane flies of which there appears to have been a population burst as a result of the recent warm spell. In a large upland lake the trout, too, are springing after the many insects that have suddenly emerged. A pair of great crested grebes together with three immature tufted ducks are swimming calmly on the open water and two families of teal are dabbling in the shallows at the far edge. An unusul show of birds for such an upland lake.

Returning home, on the verge near the lead mine, I find a freshly killed swallow. They are usually too agile to be hit by a vehicle, but this one must have been clipped, probably unprepared for traffic on this quiet backwater road. Its vivid rusty-red throat and blue-black wings and back still retain their polished sheen. Its small limp body, is unmarked and lies on the grass as if momentarily resting. It is a melancholic symbol of the dying summer.

30 AUGUST

The lambs have put on weight and lost their boisterous friskiness and the buzzards seem even more sluggish than usual. Sloth seems to have infected all living things.

I am sitting on a heathery knoll, overlooking the valley's flow. I dig my fingers into the pliant, peaty earth, and scrape up a handful. This friable mixture holds the rich aromas of the hills, of bracken, heather and damp moss. I can close my eyes and sense the throb of the mountain stream, hear tinkling bird song and feel the flutter of wings in my hand. Although I am rooted in this earth, I feel I've been temporarily loaned wings to fly and enjoy freedom's wild excess with the valley's birds for this short season.

Now the valley lies like an abandoned ship, the only sound coming from the wind in its rigging. The ash trees are laden with thick bunches of dark green keys that rattle softly and the hazels are well endowed with green-sheathed nuts. I'm more than grateful for any bird sounds at this time of year and the tick-tick alarm call of a robin in the hedge and the gentle seep-seep of a willow warbler are reassuring.

The idyll is rudely shattered by a murderous thunder exploding in the sky. Two low-flying fighter planes scream through the valley on their practice run. They utilise clear weather days for training pilots in low flying techniques. Such moments serve to remind me that peace and tranquillity are as fragile as a blackcap's nest, and it forces upon me the realisation that I am still connected to an outside world which is not so harmonious or quiet as this valley refuge is.

The low evening light filtering through the honeysuckle creates a shadow theatre on the cottage terrace. Patterns of shivering leaves are projected on to the white-washed wall and in the sun-filled interstices, bees and flies dance entranced. I watch them until the light slowly dims and gentle shadow shrouds the remains of the day.

AUTUMN

Kingfisher

A U T U M N

A utumn sidles up to summer imperceptibly, attaches itself and slowly drains the life-blood. It is invariably seen in this way: as a metaphor for dying, but I don't find it at all depressing, for me it's a colourful wake - a precondition of rebirth. I know it is only part of the renewal process and without it there could be no spring resurrection or transcendence to summer's climax.

In early autumn the trees are still full-leaved, but the winds are becoming wilder. Some leaves are already tinged with chrome and cyan. The birds have ceased singing apart from a few desultory notes from a robin or blackbird reminding us that they are still about. Fledged youngsters and adults of many other species have already formed small flocks and drifted off or begun their migrations south. Swallows and martins sit like threaded beads on telegraph wires, or flutter above, twittering animatedly, like groups of holidaying schoolchildren in anticipation of the impending trip. I can't help noticing that the birds that remain for the winter look and behave differently. Their plumage is now dulled and faded, like old, worn clothing. The tits are particularly emaciated from the rigours of the breeding season and their movements seem to lack bounce. It will take the autumn, winter and early spring for them to regain vigour and strength for the new breeding season.

The landscape changes subtly from sombre green to dull

ochre and the creeping canker of decay invades everything. Luckily death is only feigned. For some species it is a long winter sleep, for others it is merely a temporary move elsewhere. The birds of prey remain close to their breeding territories in the mountains until diminishing food supplies and the bitter cold drive them off.

6 SEPTEMBER

Today I at last get around to cleaning out the nest boxes in the alder carr by the stream. Two of the three of them were used by pied flycatchers. Here it is always dank and I'm surprised the flycatchers prefer such a damp, cool place to the dryer oak wood. The slippery path down to the stream is crawling with slugs - jet black and glutinous like slicks of tar.

Around the upper lakes there is a strip of land alongside the gorse scrub and fenced off from the sheep. Here the grass can grow long and go to seed. Small yellow flowers of tormentil glow between the desiccated stems. Flocks of meadow pipits and skylarks gather to feed on the abundant grass seed.

Four kites soar up from the hillside as I clamber over the summit of the ridge. Two of them disappear in the beech copse. In the spot they flew from a dead ram with magnificent horns, its head unblemished, lies wedged up against a fence post. The wool from its abdomen has been ripped off, exposing the bare skin stretched over the ribs like a veneer of polished mahogany. The foetid stench from the corpse hangs in the air and swarms of black flies circle a dark aperture. I continue along the ridge towards the beech copse and as I enter Snowyhead and Rusty fly out and sail over to the far side of the lake to await my departure, so that they can return to the cadaver.

Peregrine

13 SEPTEMBER

Rusty, the male red kite is patrolling the entrance to the valley, above where the river unwinds from its throat in a long white tongue. He rocks gently on the wind, like a boat in harbour. Beneath him, sheep trails zig-zag the hillsides like thin veins. Wind-shredded clouds litter the darkening sky. A buzzard sits patiently in the shelter of some gorse scrub on the hill to my left, where rabbits have honeycombed it with their burrows. The buzzard doesn't notice me approaching because its eyes are fixed on one of the burrows. Eventually a young rabbit hops out and ventures a short way down the hill and nervously sniffs the air. The buzzard waits a few seconds like a ski jumper preparing mentally for take-off. It takes wing, brushing the ground as it sails down, and pounces. The small ball of fur shakes and struggles for a few seconds then lies still. The buzzard crouches over it, clutching it firmly in its talons while cautiously monitoring the surrounding hillside.

I continue walking along the edge of a plantation and out of sight of the buzzard, leaving it to devour its kill in peace. I cross the ridge to an adjoining valley where a pair of peregrines bred successfully in the summer. I take the small road that winds up through the valley. It is hemmed in on both sides by walls of rock and scree. A flock of racing pigeons, flung over the neck of the valley like a hail of stones, careers down its whole length, then wheels round and flies back the way it's come. From out of the sky above them a speck grows larger and larger, plummeting rapidly downwards. It sprouts wings and a tail, taking on the shape of a bird, and lunges with legs extended at a straggler behind the main body of the flock. It strikes and a puff of feathers flutters from the collision. The pigeon gambols in the sky, its pinions frantically clawing the empty air, then recovers its balance as it falls and flutters towards the ground.

In the meantime the peregrine has gained height again, its strong wings rowing with clean strokes through the liquid sky, to prepare for a new attempt. It is clearly a young bird, judging by its chocolatey plumage and its botched stoop. The pigeon flies clumsily, with obvious effort, following the stream towards a small stone bridge where it disappears. I reach the bridge in a few seconds, clamber over the low dry-stone wall and down the bank of the stream and peer under its shaded arch. I find the frightened and traumatised pigeon, crouching against the stonework, small rubies of fresh blood glistening on its breast. Even my presence doesn't induce it to leave its safe refuge and face such aerial violence again.

The remainder of the flock is now flying in total confusion up and down as if imprisoned in this valley of death by some invisible force. I know I'm unable to help the pigeon and can only hope that it recovers sufficiently to escape, but I wouldn't reckon its chances as high. I'm not sentimental about killing as part of a natural food chain, but seeing this injured bird at close quarters and sensing its fear and pain, it is difficult to accept with indifference. As with the purloining of the meat we eat, most of us are content as long as we don't have to do or see the killing, but would we remain carnivorous if we had to do our own slaughtering? Death becomes acceptable when it happens at a distance or is only read about. I've certainly had my fill of killing today and am keen to seek less bloody diversion elsewhere.

Half a mile beyond the bridge, I follow the swirling waters of the stream with my eyes and glimpse a dipper feeding. It hasn't seen me approaching and stands on a boulder in the middle, looking down into the water, 'curtseying' nervously in its characteristic manner on spring-loaded legs. It then dives into the icy water, walks on the pebbly bottom for a few seconds before jumping back onto its rock, water pearling off its dark, oily plumage. I can clearly see the glaucoma-like nictitating membrane, which covers its eyes, facilitating vision, while it is feeding under water. It feeds like this a number of times before shooting off downstream and under the bridge, ignoring the pigeon still cowering there.

15 SEPTEMBER

The sun silvers the farm roofs in the valley and they glisten through the milky swirl below the pools which lie cast on the hills like fallen shards of sky. The lane is smoky with the early mist, but it soon clears. Some early autumn days are sunnier and warmer than many a one in summer and today is one of these. There is not the slightest zephyr and the brittle leaves hang lifeless on the trees like twists of dry, sloughed skin. The sun throbs in a clear sky. Light floods through the thinning foliage, freckling the ground, tanning the bark of the pines a ruddy orange and back-lighting the ginger tousle of dead bracken.

Large swarms of midges and a few butterflies flutter in the hedge, while flies, still drugged with sleep, hum lethargically around the farm outbuildings. It is like a summer's day. The mistle thrushes, animated by the warmth, are yodeling from the tree tops and entranced buzzards twirl over the valley on the warm uplift.

1 OCTOBER

Today I feel the need to leave the quiet womb of the valley, to be infected again by the restlessness of the sea and to be deafened by its roar.

There is only a light breeze wafting in, but the sea itself is quite turbulent, heaving large breakers onto the shore, making sea watching almost impossible as any birds on the water disappear in the deep troughs that follow each wave. The sea is the colour of wet concrete, except at the horizon, where the sun has broken through the low cloud, laying a girdle of glinting silver around the distant waist of the smudged mountains.

Male stonechat and whinchat

Light shimmers across the shore, which is bare apart from a scattering of gulls, motionless, like white pebbles cast on the wet sand. Two oystercatchers balance one-legged on their own inverted reflections, while three ringed plovers, the only apparently animate objects, scuttle back and forth at the sea's edge.

Where the river debouches into the sea, on the sandy shore there is an exposed bed of large pebbles and only as I get very close to it do I realise that I have been looking at one of those optical puzzles, where, if you squint long enough at what is seemingly a flat, random pattern, three dimensional figures begin to emerge from the background. As soon as I am within 40 metres, a flock of around 100 golden plover in winter plumage separates out from the real stones. They are crouching, their heads facing the breeze, absolutely still. They allow me to approach without showing any sign of alarm at all. Among them are about fifty small dunlin, as invisible as the plovers, unless I use binoculars. I walk past, but as if I had awoken them from a deep trance, they suddenly rise in a whirlwind of glittering white and gold, circle once or twice, before coalescing into a rough 'V' to fly inland to feed in the flooded fields. Every year a flock of between 100 and 150 golden plovers gathers in the vicinity of the estuary, often in this same spot. The camouflage of the stones probably affords them protection from predators. I'm not sure where they come from, certainly not from the local moors where their numbers are down to very few pairs.

In the dunes, a single male stonechat sits dejectedly on top of a bramble bush, obviously not enjoying the blustery weather. He valiantly clutches the rocking stem with his slender legs, desperate to keep a balance in the gusts. But he does bring a small splash of colour to the bleak surroundings. Despite the cutting wind, I continue walking around the estuary and onto the dyke wall, holding the channel which drains flood waters from the low-lying fields. A small, dark ball of feathers slides into the oily depths of the flood channel beside the dyke and disappears. It is a little grebe investigating new feeding grounds away from its breeding site. I think there is no other life around until a glint of colour catches my eye. A bright jewel flashes among the trailing twigs of a weeping willow and a kingfisher, disturbed while fishing, shoots off down stream, like a fleeing fragment of rainbow, its brilliant plumage momentarily illuminated as it speeds past a bank of dark rhododendrons and is caught by the sun. Dense swarms of midges swirl like vapour over the still waters. Within the hour the sun gutters and is gone, sunk into the deep velvet of the hills, leaving a few embers weakly glowing in the grate of the night.

18 OCTOBER

The early morning sky is bright and clear like a polished wine glass. The round, communion wafer of moon is floating still on the pink-blue tongue of the sky. The extremities of the firs and oaks are edged with a golden glow by the October sun and there is not a tremble of wind. The unseasonable warmth has brought out tortoiseshell and cabbage white butterflies in the heather and dragon flies are skimming the reeds around the small flood pools.

Although it is pleasantly warm and tranquil, the recent storm-driven sea has left dirty tide marks of flotsam on the coastal fields which are still sodden. The assorted plastic bottles, tins and polystyrene vandalise the landscape with their reminder of urban squalor.

The salt marsh lies like an enormous wet, moulting pelt on the landscape. At its slimy extremities water birds feeding on the rich silt are strung out like loose strings of beads. Around 100 lapwings and a similar number of curlews are resting among the stubbly reed and a single sandpiper, like a brown mouse, scurries along the river bank. It appears to have missed the general exodus south. As I stand watching this tranquil scene, the birds suddenly rise and whirl in seeming panic as if a shot had been fired which only I had not heard. I realise they must have been alarmed by something, so I scan the sky. There, arrowing from the trees and out over the salt marsh is a peregrine falcon, scrutinising the birds to pick out a weaker or less careful member of the flock. It doesn't find one, but perhaps it has already fed, so maintains its determined flight down the coast and I lose it in the distance.

There are six shelduck, their heads down and oscillating sideways, back and forth, sifting through the silt. They are probably from the local population - the migrants from the north have not yet arrived. A small party of teal whiffles down from the sky in a short shower to land in a flurry of wings and splash of water on a small flood pool. In a flock of over two hundred Canada geese feeding on the soft turf, I'm thrilled to discover four smaller barnacle geese hiding. Large flocks of wigeon are paddling in the soft mud and there is also a small party of pintail. The decorative males with their dark chocolate heads mounted on long necks are peeking above the rushes, keeping a watchful eye on me.

19 OCTOBER

Another warm day. Our 'summer' is certainly late this year, but wonderful nevertheless.

The small, quiet harbour in the town provides bathing and resting facilities for flocks of black-headed gulls, and the rocks around the harbour wall offer good feeding for small parties of turnstones. These small, friendly waders arrive from the north in the autumn and remain around the rocky areas of coast before returning north again in the spring. They are often quite difficult to discern as their mottled plumage merges with the colours of the olive bladder wrack and wet rocks. They use their strong, slightly retrousse beaks to turn over the pebbles, an activity which has given them their name, to find the small molluscs and crustacea hiding beneath. As I watch, several of them throw even large stones into the air, like miniature shot-putters, and creating a loud clatter. They are quite oblivious of my watching them from the sea wall only a few meters away. Others are resting, like holidaying pensioners snatching a snooze, their heads tucked cosily into their dorsal plumage. A single redshank, as if in need of company, has joined their small party. Below these, three dusky rock pipits, those all-year-round coastal residents, chase sand flies, tempted out of the tangled knots of damp seaweed by the warm sun.

The flat coast curves around the bay, to rise steeply in a volcano-shaped hill. It is dark and forbidding on its seaward side and brilliant green on its landward. Mixed parties of corvids are foraging there for larvae and worms in the short sward. Along the coastal path small clumps of hardy Japanese Rose bushes have established themselves. Their bright scarlet hips are fat and juicy, providing a rich food source for flocks of greenfinches and linnets. Their beaks are running with orange juice as they tear at the soft skins. On the beach seven ringed plovers are resting, their heads buried in their backs, but their eyes remain open and watchful. Several are clearly juveniles, lacking the characteristic dark breast ring.

Where the flat beach gives way to large rocks and cliffs, the bird life changes. Oystercatchers, like soldiers guarding the outposts, stand alert on the rock ledges, piping their alarm if they see anything untoward. A peregrine tiercel makes a mock stoop at a raven flying close to the cliff, but swerves away shortly before impact and disappears behind the cliff face. There is always rivalry between these birds for the few suitable cliff ledges, but as ravens nest much earlier, they usually get their way and the peregrines have to make do with the ravens' old nest or a second class ledge. Two kestrels are winnowing together over the cliff top – a juvenile and an adult male – their eyes filtering the landscape for movement. One or two are always to be found nesting on the cliffs, but the stronger peregrine has priority over territory.

Five great black-backed gulls crouch like elegant vultures on a large upturned plate of rock, their anthracite-coloured backs contrasting sharply with their starched white heads and breasts. Below them, perfectly camouflaged are two grey seals, sunbathing on a narrow rock ledge.

The sea is clearly not as vacuous as it appears. As I sit and peer down from my vertiginous outpost, two groups of dolphins, quite close to the cliff, break the surface with their dorsal fins. Two of them play in the shallower waters just below me and I can follow their pale grey, shadowy forms as they twist and turn in the clear water, their flukes slapping the surface. The other three are darker and one has a white scar on its fin and nose, as if it has been attacked by a shark or slashed by a ship's propeller.

The cliffs here rise up steeply from the sea in sinuate strata of sedimentary rock, evidence of the tumultuous geological birth this coastland underwent. It is these strata and the asynchronous eroding of them, which have provided the ledges for the colonies of seabirds that nest here in spring.

20 OCTOBER

Today there is a change in wind direction and a strong South-westerly drives water-laden clouds in from the Atlantic. Pale grey cumulus surges relentlessly across the sky and brings sudden, heavy squalls that drive the buzzards and kites down from the heavens to shelter. The fields become saturated, the birds remain hidden in the sheltering foliage and insects creep into crevices. Only the slugs and snails relish the new moistness and venture out to feed avidly on the succulent vegetation. Heavy droplets cling, then slip down the window panes imposing sequined patterns on the coarse weave of sodden green which now covers the patient hills. The droplet-laden grass, glistens and sparkles in the keen light. The inundation is so heavily that I half expect to see dolphins plunging over the hills.

A buzzard is perched in the ash tree, pressing against the trunk in an attempt to escape the downpour. As I fetch firewood from the terrace it inclines its head slightly, hardly deigning to note my presence, but remains glued to its niche. The tonsured mountains rising behind it appear to cringe under the icy rain lashing their obeisant, bared backs. The sullen sky clings to the mountain tops refusing to be dislodged.

One of the joys of British weather, if one wishes to see it positively, is its unpredictability and changeability: hot, sunny days transmuting into wet and misty ones, oppressive grey giving way to heady blue, tranquility shattered by blustery bursts. But today I find it hard to be positive and fret indoors, impatient for the rain to cease. A fruitless day in terms of observations for the diary, but the rain has cleansed the air, leaving it silky-soft.

21 OCTOBER

After the heavy rains in the night, I awake to a Chinese landscape of mist-wreathed hills, punctured by the blurred silhouettes of fir trees, like minarets above the swirling grey. The mist drifts up the valley like the breath of some huge mountain dragon. All animal life is hidden. It is impossible to do any bird watching until it clears.

The afternoon produces change, but not the one expected. The few previous days of the postponed summer are well and truly shattered by buffeting winds and icy showers. Big-bosomed clouds race across the sky and the few remaining leaves are torn from the trees and tossed in the maelstrom.

Hereabouts the lanes are very narrow and the hedge-banks high, reflecting the decades of use by drovers carts. This constant use has worn away the soil and the lanes have sunk beneath the surrounding land. When the hedges are in full leaf, one is cut off from the landscape as if trapped in a labyrinth. In early summer their steep banks are covered in a profusion of primroses, stitchworts and other wild flowers, but now they are bare. The hedges, too, are bedraggled and melancholic, almost devoid of birds. A solitary dunnock sits on a hazel and clicks at me, while three magpies are tossed over the hedge into the field by the wind. As I turn the corner while wandering along such a sunken lane, only a few miles from the valley I think I've strayed accidently into Peru. Peering at me over the hedge are two brown, wooly-clad alpacas! I'm used to sheep in the hills, but not being confronted by South American immigrants. There are four of them altogether and they appear to be perfectly happy in this damp, hilly environment. Their luxurious wool will no doubt be more lucrative for the farmer than a sheep's fleece.

The low evening sun caresses the valley, arousing its rich tapestry of autumnal hues: the rusts, ochres and auburns. Its light falls steeply from the high hills, sliding gently to the flatter meadows below. It retreats slowly, draining the colour from the valley cleft, leaving it a joyless and empty place for the night to take possession. As the light dims, a small flock of fieldfares on winter wings flicker above the house and then plunge to the shelter of a firwood in the valley below. These harbingers of winter are the first I've seen and their presence brings a palpable chill to the air.

22 OCTOBER

The night brings a considerable drop in temperature and in the morning the strawberry plants are coated with a white, granular patina of frost.

The day conveys the distinct impression that a handover from autumn to winter is taking place. A gale rips into the countryside. The vegetation, already scorched by the recent bitterly cold winds, is now being battered into submission. The valley's small stream, usually crystal clear, is the colour of milky coffee as its already silt-laden waters continue to tear at the banks.

On the coast the air is brittle and clear. The enraged sea flings itself at the coast, depositing capuccino-coloured foam onto the beach. Wraith-like scarves of sand granules are driven across it so that its whole expanse appears to be in movement.

The estuary lies wide and flat, like a scorched pancake tossed beneath the hills. From this distance it appears to be devoid of all life. I wander along the single-line railway track which traverses its monotone expanse. There is indeed little activity to be seen. A few pairs of mallard are paddling along the muddy banks of the creek and a female merganser swims strongly downstream, nervous of my presence. Beyond it, in the distance, my eye is caught by a duck-like bird with large white wing patches. It is not a goosander and doesn't fit the pattern of any other duck I'm familiar with. My curiosity aroused, I creep towards it, shielded by the tall bed of phragmites reed that grows profusely by the river here and in late spring resounds to the animated chattering of sedge and reed warblers, like a school class when the teacher is out. Now only the rattle and scratching of the dry reed stalks abrades the silence.

Eventually I estimate I am close enough to emerge onto the open river bank for a closer view of this strange bird. I am lucky, it is still squatting on the mud. I raise my binoculars and my 'rarity' is suddenly transformed into a pied muscovy duck! Disappointment turns to amusement as I realise how gullible I've been. As I stand there humbled by my fallibility, my attention is diverted by a rotund figure in seaman's cap bearing down on me along the track. He has emerged from a small cottage which I hadn't seen as it is obscured by shrubbery.

I think he is about to upbraid me for trespassing, but he asks amicably if I'm bird watching. On hearing my affirmative, he becomes really loquacious. He used to be a deputy headmaster, he tells me, in a big inner-London comprehensive school. After seeing one of his colleagues die of a heart attack and others go off on long-term sick due to stress, he decided, even though only in his early fifties, to get out before he too succumbed, and to return to his roots. He now lives in this small signalman's cottage marooned blissfully in the middle of the estuary salt flats, with no road access and only two small coastal trains a day to disturb his peace. He is a bird watcher himself and he tells me what he's seen on the estuary. Only the week before there was a flock of around 2,000 wigeon feeding on the marshes and at night he hears fieldfares, redwing and small flocks of godwits flying over his cottage. More excitingly, he says he has had a resident spoonbill on the river as well as receiving visits from little egrets on a regular basis, but I am not privileged to see any of these today. As so often with birds and animals, it is a question of timing and good luck. I have to be content with several piping redshank and a small party of wigeon. He has, however, corrected my impression of this area as a desert.

As I return home, I am again struck by the placid beauty and tonal mutability of this valley and I never tire of its view. It stretches away below me in a tesselated corridor of small fields, towards a horizon already misting into a blur as the evening cools. The bracken is rusting at the edges like a tin can; the woodland fringes are already browned and yellowed and in the following days this will spread like a contagion into the heartlands.

While walking down, past the edge of the fir plantation behind the house, I hear tearing and crackling sounds high in one of the crowns. I stop beneath the tree and look up, curious to see what is making the noise, expecting to see a squirrel. High up, the tree is adorned with a rich fringe of large, pendulent cones. Clinging to them and tearing with abandon at their tough scales are several crossbills. There are two rosy-pink males and three grey-green females. Their misaligned mandibles, cleverly perfected for prising pine kernels from their scaly integuments, rip the inedible pieces from the cones, scattering the litter like confetti on the ground around me. They are so intent on their task that they ignore my presence below and I am able to watch them for several minutes before they move deeper into the wood and I'm left with a painful crick in my neck. Crossbills are just one of the species that have benefitted from the spread of plantations over the Welsh hills, but are not easy birds to see. They are often to be found deep in the woods, high in the crowns where the cones are concentrated. They are easier to spot in small flocks, identified by their stubby plump shape and characteristic wheezy, twittering calls.

The hawthorns are heavy with bunches of dark wine-red berries, awaiting the invasion of northern thrushes. I'm able to fill my pockets with hazel nuts from the hedges behind the cottage, wading through the yellow spear-heads of ash leaves which litter the field margins. Invariably the squirrels beat me to it and have denuded the bushes before the nuts have had a chance to mature; this year it is obviously a bountiful crop and enough for both squirrels and me!

24 OCTOBER

I utilise an obligatory shopping visit to the town to do a little bird watching around the harbour and the adjoining coast.

I spot four ringed plovers feeding among the algae on the harbour rocks together with two turnstones. Out at sea one or two common scoter are riding the waves - the first outriders of the bigger flocks that will arrive later.

In the rain-soaked fields near the coast, a flock of around 200 golden plovers is resting - some of them possibly the same birds I saw earlier. Their summer gold now tarnished and dulled to pale yellow. With them is a similar number of lapwing. As the light dwindles and I am about to call it a day and leave for home, I spot a large grey wraith of a bird flapping low over a dyke on the skyline: a male hen harrier - the first of the autumn - is out hunting for voles or small birds. I follow his flight until he drops beneath the bank and is lost. I know I will encounter him again during the winter as he wanders over the flat coastal area and marshland. He will soon be joined by other males and young birds leaving the high moors where they've spent the summer. The stronger females tend to stay on the moors longer, where they can survive on a diet of larger prey, like rabbits and grouse.

25 OCTOBER

A bright sunny day. The sky is as brittle as a dunnock's egg and of the same clear lapis blue. The kite pair is circling lazily over the valley and they are stooping playfully at each other. A buzzard is cruising higher up and mewing plaintively. Through binoculars I can see its beak opening as it calls.

I trim back the wild tentacles of the honeysuckle around the door of the cottage, before it occludes my entrance completely. While I'm doing this, a robin and wren hold a low-key conversation under the spruces and a goldcrest pair diligently comb the crowns for food. Already small green spikes of crocuses are poking through on the rockery. The sheep are taciturn - too preoccupied with building up their fat reserves for the winter to waste energy on vocal expression.

A weariness seems to have taken hold; the wild summer hedonism has drained life's energies. The lethargy is infectious and today I too feel no strong desire to leave my domicile, but choose instead to potter about, doing those jobs which require urgent attention before the onset of winter.

3 NOVEMBER

The hills have now been weathered to a dull rust where the dead bracken lies prostrate, the oaks in the valley woods are bare, exposing their moss and lichen encrusted limbs to the outside world, and the birch buds on their slender twigs lend the glades a dark purple sheen. The winds have wrapped scarves of crisp leaves around the woodland edges.

The wood behind the cottage is like an empty school playground, apart from a pair of jays, noisy like drunken janitors and the distant cheeping from small parties of tits or goldcrests as they forage in the crowns of the firs, higher up. By the lakes a male reed bunting chinks from a willow tree and small groups of linnets and a charm of goldfinches flicker in the gorse. A buzzard flaps across to the wood and my first flock of redwings this year sweeps up from the ground into a tall ash tree and chunter in annoyance as I draw near. As they fly the ruddy axillaries under their wings, glimmer like glowing coals. Their markings lend them a more graphic appearance than our resident song and mistle thrushes, whose plumage is of a lighter brown and the spots and striations softer.

The needle-littered floor of the firwood is like a soft and springy mattress underfoot. It makes no sound as I patter, feline-like, past the scabrous trunks of pines, reeking of resin which mingles with the autumnal scent of decaying wood and leafmold. Descending along a straggly hawthorn hedge, towards the valley bottom, my attention is caught by a male sparrowhawk, flying low over the ground and into the wood ahead of me. I follow it and search the now leafless trees for a sign of the bird, which I'm sure hasn't left the wood. Looking up at the twig-veined sky, I soon locate him. I can just make out his slim form, hugging the trunk of a larch, static and hardly visible, trying to avoid discovery by small birds which would mob it. It knows up there it's safe from me and doesn't even make to fly. A little group of, striated, lemony siskins scamper from fir to fir, only metres away from the hawk and clearly unaware of its presence, so still does it sit.

A loud banging draws me to a tall lime tree and I follow the trunk upwards with my eyes. I expect to see a great spotted woodpecker or large jay, but am amazed to find that a tiny nuthatch is producing the sound. It is pecking with all its might on a hollow branch like a woodpecker, its legs splayed to provide a firm grip and using its whole body as a hammer, ramming its beak into the wood, like a demented percussionist.

As I leave the wood, the wind lifts up the dry leaves, wheeling them round like a flock of birds, then drops them down again. The dead oak leaves still clinging to the twigs cackle as the wind rushes past. Jays from the sombre depths of the firs behind me suddenly squeal like pigs being slaughtered, although there appears to be no outward reason for their clamour.

4 NOVEMBER

The air is tingling cold, but the hanging sun glints promisingly under an azure sky, scarred only faintly by a few bands of cirrus.

On the estuary 25 whitefronted geese, all the way from Greenland, nuzzle at the short grass. Mergansers - all red-heads - are playing an avian version of 'tag' on the river, while a group of oystercatchers watch bemused from the bank.

As I wander along the hedge by the river, a large flock of tits

Great spotted woodpeckers

- blue and coal, but mostly long-tailed - are pinging through a line of dwarf birches, driven by hunger and the shortness of the days to restless foraging. The thripping of the long-taileds follows me as I continue along the path. I'm convinced that a succession of mild winters has been a boon to these birds. They are one of the very few species which seem to have become more numerous since my boyhood days.

The oaks, now completely denuded, crouch stiff-limbed on the frigid slopes that rise from the river valley. In their tracery, last year's nests are exposed to view - the many crows' and magpies', but also those of the buzzards and kites. I'm always interested at this time of year to discover which breeding birds in the area I've missed. I find an untidy bullfinch's nest in old Evans's orchard hedge, a neat goldfinch's in the neighbour's Cyprus leylandi and a dunnock's mossy cup in the bramble thicket in the lane by the gate.

The only birds which seem almost to relish this time of year and remain doggedly on the hills, are the ravens. It's not surprising that the raven has been granted mystical status in many folklore traditions. It is a very intelligent, versatile and resilient bird. Here in Wales the population is one of the largest in the world. The bird's deep bass honking is sometimes the only animal sound to be heard over the moors and crags and helps dispel the fear and sense of isolation. Having a raven around is almost like having a pet. It underlines one's fragile existence and that brittle bond between human beings and the natural world. As I enter the front door a pair flies over, heading for their roost in the plantation, grunting with apparent anticipation of a night's rest.

9 NOVEMBER

I awake to a clear sky, suffused with morning pink. A full, goat's milk moon floats high over the hills which are bathed in a soft golden glow by the November sun. A light frost has left a fine crystal rime on the brambles. I miss the swathes of succulent green bracken that in summer clothed the hillsides around the cottage. Now there are only rusty patches where it stood.

The afternoon brings rain-laden clouds rolling off the hills. The sharp showers rip the few remaining leaves from the trees and hedges. With the foliage gone, I can again see the lane which has become a wet, glistening serpent, slithering down between the hills, its head lost in the woods below. The countryside seems listless and somnolent. The lachrymose trees are tapping out a percussive crescendo on the leaf litter as they shed the superfluous water.

I ignore the rain and take a stroll up the lane. A mile up the

Ravens

valley, beyond the lead mine there is a windowless farm house with a rusting hay binder parked in front, as if its former occupants had upped and left in a hurry. Nettles are growing up through its iron wheels. As I pass it a dozen jackdaws explode from the crumbling roof eaves, cackling like old crones. I feel it would be an ideal site for a barn owl, but they are scarce in the area and the odd birds that we have tend to frequent the lower valley, where there are hay meadows, hedges and bigger farms.

Only on rare occasions, when it rains almost incessantly for days and the granite skies hang immovably above, do I feel cowed. As a rule the weather doesn't engender that sense of desolation it would in a large city. Here it serves to accentuate the natural features of the landscape. It intensifies the greenness and increases the turbulence and velocity of the streams, forging the will to survive in the face of adversity. That's why the kites, buzzards and peregrines have survived here. They have been hardened and their resilience is tested to its limits.

Clambering up the steep, scree-strewn mountainside is arduous. My feet slip and slide, dislodging stones. There is a danger of sliding down with them, but I'm determined to reach the summit which will give me a buzzard's eye view the length of the valley. At the far end, there is a rocky outcrop which held a peregrine's eyrie in spring. The birds, though, have probably left the valley for the coast by now.

While looking for clumps of heather or bilberry to grab and pull myself up, I see it lying, wedged against a rock. Its eyes are dark, empty holes, its talons dull straw colour, gripping the air in rigor mortis and its rapier-sharp beak is clamped shut. The dark brown plumage tells me it's a first year bird. There are no obvious clues as to how it died - no shot wounds nor wire around its legs. It may have been poisoned by eating tainted bait put out by a farmer for foxes, but I'll never know. A dead peregrine is a rare and sad sight. I find it difficult to imagine such a strong, athletic bird cut down before its first year is out. I'm so used to thinking of the peregrine as the cause of death, not its victim. I leave it lying, like a piece of driftwood, stiff and brittle, flung there by the wind. It remains the only peregrine I see the whole day. As I stumble back down through the scree, spokes of sunlight radiate from beneath the low layer of cloud, bathing the late afternoon moor in a soft pale ochre, fitting my melancholy and pensive mood.

16 NOVEMBER

The raised bog in autumn and winter is always a good place to see birds of prey. They come here in a greater number and variety at this time of year, obviously finding it a rewarding place in terms of hunting.

When I arrive in late afternoon, kites are gathering and spiral in tight circles over an old sheep's carcass, competing with two buzzards as well as a motley crew of crows and magpies. As the kites circle, light from the low-lying sun is filtered through their translucent primaries and tail feathers, spinning them into woven gold; where the feathers overlap they are darker. The kites mob the crows, like skuas do terns, forcing them to relinquish their morsels, then pounce to grasp the meat as it falls.

Kites are undoubtedly the masters of the air, wheeling, braking and bombing. Using their tails like rudders and their long, slender wings as flexible oars, they out-manoeuvre all other avian scavengers.

In spring and summer I'm easily torn out of any melancholic torpor, borne along by the torrent of new activity, the continual arrival of bird visitors, the outpouring of song and the cascades of floral colour. Early autumn is leavened by sunny days and the chromatic changes of the decaying foliage. But late autumn is like a house clearance after the departure or death of a dear friend. You are left behind in an almost empty house, confronted by bare walls and shelves where once loved objects stood, and with only a few hanging curtains still left. There is scarce a sound and you know it will be a long wait before the rooms are furnished and peopled again. You look at the chairs in which your friends so recently sat, the table where they ate, their animated conversation only a faint echo in your head. The valley feels like that now and I miss these companions with whom I experienced so much pleasure and enjoyment.

Even the old lead workings appear more gaunt and depressingly deserted than earlier in the year, and the steady drizzle only serves to compound the sense of loss. I retreat to my refuge, where at least the licking flames of a log fire can compensate somewhat for the drabness, lack of colour and warmth outside.

WINTER

Teal pair

WINTER

Winter can easily convert solitude into loneliness, contemplation into melancholy. The days are short, the sun only a cursory visitor. The sea is often locked in violent battle with rampaging storms. The mountains become containing walls and the trees barred windows to an unfriendly sky. Many resident birds seem to shun the valley in winter and it provides a foreboding of what it could be like in spring and summer too if the countryside were allowed to go the way of East Anglia or the Midlands where we've created agricultural cemeteries. Massed flocks of avian visitors once darkened the skies over the fens and wetlands, now too often only empty vistas greet the eye; where bird song cascaded from every hedgerow, there is now a deathly hush. Our greed and hubris has driven the birds hence.

Here winter is a particularly unpredictable and capricious season. One minute it can be surprisingly warm and sunny, the next bitterly cold. Moorland which is frozen and walkable one minute becomes a sodden, treacherous place the next. Wild storms alternate with mild breezes, clear skies with driving mist and rain. This year is one like that. It's not only that I don't know what to wear from one day to the next, but it is also difficult to prepare psychologically for the unexpected swings. The days are in any case short, so decisions can't be made with dilatory equivocation, if I want to take full advantage of the few daylight hours.

The cold winter winds, the rain, sleet and snow drive virtually all animal life from the moors, to seek more hospitable accommodation in the sheltered valleys or on the coast.

To wander the hills at this time of year is often pure masochism; it is to offer oneself to the brutal lash of the wild wind, as it races unchecked over the bare-backed summits. And on such days one concurs with King Lear when he bemoans:

"poor naked wretches, whereso'er you are,
that bide the pelting of this pitiless storm,
how shall your houseless heads and unfed sides,
your loop'd and window'd raggedness defend you
from seasons such as these?"

No wonder these hills are marked everywhere by the remnants and ruins of abandoned dwellings.

The long winter evenings provide an ideal opportunity to reflect on and review the past year, and in doing so memories of even further back are awakened. Any countryside experience I have today irresistibly brings comparisons with the past. My fondest memories are of bird nesting exploits as a young boy - something that would quite rightly be frowned on today because of the damage it can cause, particularly to our rarer breeding birds. But at that time the lanes, woods and hedges seemed to throb with birds, and our activities didn't have any obvious effect on numbers at all. We must have caused a number of birds to desert by taking their eggs for our collections, but the impact was probably minimal compared with the destruction caused by modern agricultural techniques and urban spread. We would spend hours on end wandering country lanes and over fields, oblivious of time. There would be robins' nests every hundred yards or so in the hedge banks and we learned to spot the tell-tale platform of dead leaves which formed the entrance to the nest. Common whitethroats churred from every patch of cow parsley and bramble thicket. Yellow hammers sang from the telegraph wires and grey partridges sat tight on their large clutches of khaki-coloured eggs beneath the hedges. It was an idyllic time and we would wander as if drugged by the heady scent of dog roses and meadowsweet, reluctant to acknowledge the day's close. Back home we'd proudly display our bloodied arms and faces and battered knees - the wounds of battle received shinning up trees and clambering through thorn bushes after nests. There were few cars on the roads and the only real dangers were being chased by frisky bullocks in a field or of falling into ponds when dangling over the water on slender willow branches while looking for moorhens' nests.

I've been interested in birds and the countryside for as far back as I can remember. I joined the Royal Society for the Protection of Birds as a youngster in the Fifties, when its membership could be counted in a few hundred and bird watchers were still viewed as rather eccentric. I went to conferences and to RSPB reserves and met many of the leading bird experts of the day. I also became one of the BTO's youngest accredited ringers. Then came a long period of living and working in a large city and my binoculars were left to gather dust in the cupboard until the red kites of the valleys rekindled my passion.

18 DECEMBER

Today I'm alone on the high moor with the storm's bellowing and rushing, picking my way cautiously between clumps of damp rush, squelching beds of sphagnum moss, peat pools and rushing rivulets. I find myself perched on what seems to be the rim of the planet, at the mercy of the sky raging around me, threatening to pitch me headlong over the cliff or drown me in icy rain, determined to purge its domain of my intrusive presence. Winter is not a hospitable time on the mountain tops, the valleys are kinder. I stagger on down the slope. The crowded hills part as I get closer and let me through, only to close in again behind me. They glower and threaten, but then all of a sudden retreat, exposing an open valley before me.

Almost from under my feet a lone snipe rockets into the air and zig-zags over the marsh to plunge down into dense reed several hundred meters away. I am not alone after all! It had clearly been feeding in the flooded terrain before I disturbed it. The few dunlins and golden plovers to be found in the area left these inhospitable heights weeks ago to join their fellows from Scotland and Scandinavia on the food-rich coastal plains. They were followed by the peregrines and merlins, who vanish from the crags and moors in winter, as do many of the pipits and skylarks, to seek refuge in the milder valleys and on the coast. The kites drift and scavenge ever further from their nest sites, returning to visit every so often. Only the buzzards tend to hang around their old territories, although even they will avoid the higher altitudes in inclement weather.

I too am glad to be back in the shelter of the valley as the late afternoon temperature drops and the pallid sun retreats to the west, leaving a nacreous sky suffused with pink. A flock of starlings, like a synchronised swarm of locusts, funnels down the valley towards the milder coast as the night seeps into the crevices between the hills.

23 DECEMBER

The bitterly cold easterly is still scouring the hills. It hasn't yet brought snow, but has fringed the riverbanks with icy lace and forged the water dribbling off the hills into spears of ice. Its force is muted in the shelter of the hills.

The two ridges enclosing the valley are smooth, rounded and bare, like two enormous barrows. The woods huddle in the folds and crinkles. Plaits of water cascade from the summits. In the lower valley the berry-laden hawthorns and rowans are throbbing with ravenous fieldfare and redwing, flown in from northern and eastern Europe on the prevailing winds and now replenishing energy stores. Hawthorns and rowans are probably the most typical scrub trees of mid-Wales and although often small of stature, produce abundant berries, essential for such winter visitors. On frosty mornings like this one, when the wind has spent its force, it seems that almost every other telegraph pole along the narrow lanes possesses a feathered extension, puffed up buzzards sit immobile like statues carved from the poles themselves. Imperiously, they survey the surrounding land with their all-seeing eyes for any indication of movement or easy pickings from a 'kill' on the road. They are determined to conserve energy in these low temperatures.

A robin flies up from the field onto the terrace with obvious effort. Its tail looks bulbous and is clearly pulling the bird down. On examining it through binoculars I can see a large clump of ice fixed solidly to its tail feathers. As it roosted during the night water must have dripped onto its tail and then frozen. I can only hope that the day's sun will engender sufficient warmth to melt the ice and release the poor bird from its burden.

For the naturalist, winter makes life easier in many ways. The cold obliges animals to come out and hunt more often and the lack of foliage cover exposes whole panoramas to prying eyes. Hares bound over the frozen ground, stoats with black-tipped tails scuttle across the paths and down the hedge banks, and foxes on the prowl for careless pheasants instinctively hug the hedgerows, even though these offer scant cover, .

I scan the sky above the hills: they are empty, but for a magpie crossing languorously from one copse to another. I know the kite pair will not be far away, maybe in the adjacent valley or resting in one of the big oaks, eyeing me through their socketed circles of chrome. After breeding, and once the young are mature enough to forage for themselves, the pair may disperse quite far from the nesting area, but will always return at regular intervals, as if to keep an eye on their territory. Autumn and winter are the best times to see kites. Carrion becomes scarcer during the winter months, making the search a full-time occupation and keeping the birds on the move. They are less secretive in their movements and traverse greater distances while hunting.

The valley becomes silent in winter, like a deserted beach after the summer holidays. Only the unrhythmic throb of the wind and gushing of the stream provide aural evidence of the natural world. Even the sheep in the fields are quieted. Low cloud and mist have settled over the surrounding hills, creating an island, removing geographical perspective and the reassurance of connectedness. The trees, like monumental totems to an interred summer, pattern this now sacred place. Scabs of dead and prostrate bracken cling to the green and ochre skin of the slopes, like sores on a corpse.

24 DECEMBER

The morning sky is still marred by the dark dregs of night, but already the hunters are up and about. Two kites, probably Rusty and Snowyhead - I can't be sure from this distance - are following the curve of the hill top, then glide down into the valley. Over the hay meadows they indulge in pair bonding, demonstrating an almost palpable joy at today's spring-like weather. They play dive and fly pick-a-back, then lock talons in the air, tumbling, before parting to regain height. Rusty drifts over towards the oakwood where she may nest, Snowyhead continues circling up the valley, before being eclipsed by a hill, like a gull behind a large wave.

There is more activity around human habitations than on the bare hills, because they usually offer more ready food sources. Great and blue tits, several at a time, flit onto the terrace, take kernels from the feeder and fly off with them into the hedge. They first land on the twigs of an old ash branch I've cut down and laid against the wall, take stock and then spring up to the feeder. Chaffinches potter about picking up the seeds scattered with profligate abandon by the tits, and a curious blackbird arrives to see what's on offer. I've also split some walnuts and scattered them on the paving stones. One of the tits holds the hull of half a walnut with its foot and with short sharp stabs attacks the soft kernel inside. There is a continuous coming and going; a sort of avian fly-in fast food outlet among the shards of plant pots, cracked and broken by the year's frosts. A male great spotted woodpecker repeats his sharp chit-chit from the top of a nearby larch, his crimson nape and under-tail coverts are picked out in the clear light, as he clambers up the trunk using his stiff tail as a third leg.

The hedge alongside the track to the cottage and adjoining field was trimmed by the farmer last month. In summer it was alive with tits, flycatchers, warblers and robins, its high growth of hazel and ash offering good protection and food. Now it looks like a badly shorn and mutilated sheep. No longer are hedges lovingly and skillfully coppiced, laid and interlaced to provide thick and sturdy growth; they are flayed by machine, leaving messy, torn and frayed ends, in which fungus spores find easy purchase, thus speeding the hedge's demise. But I suppose we are lucky to have a hedge still - many around have been grubbed out and replaced by monotonous, standard fencing. Technological progress, unfortunately, so often equals rural unemployment and destruction of country life. For every mechanised hedge cutter or binder two or more jobs are lost and another cottage falls into disrepair and is eventually abandoned. For the birds and animals, too, it means reduced habitat.

25 DECEMBER

The wind has now eased and the clouds drawn back, revealing a clear blue proscenium of ceramic blue, lit by a pallid winter sun. I make an early start so that I can get in a good walk before attempting to conquer the Christmas dinner. Although it is still very cold, it's pleasant out as long as I'm well wrapped up. No more streaming eyes and nose and frost-bitten fingers!

A walk through the forestry plantations that flank the lower valley, provides shelter from the intermittent gusts. Here I am enveloped in a satin silence; the thick folds and pleats of the firs seem to absorb all sound. Only the dull crunch of my own boots on the flinty path and the muted seep-seep calls of goldcrests in the fir crowns add rhythm to the whisperings of the wind. It is difficult to envisage that these same woodlands contained so much life only a few months ago.

As I reach the far end of the valley the woods again open out onto bare hills and their sparse covering of grass affords grazing for a small flock of sheep. In a sheltered dell, alongside two ancient ash trees, are the ruins of a small farmer's cottage and out-buildings. Only the walls are still standing with tufts of harts-tongue, maidenhair fern and navelwort growing out of the crevices between the stones. It is a memorial to those who for generations eked a living from these unkind hills, until the elements proved too resilient and overpowered them. The damp hills rise steeply behind it like a wave threatening to engulf the last evidence of human hubris. The outer walls are crumbling and nettles proliferate around the entrance. The roof is bowed like the upturned hull of a boat and, where the heavy slates have slipped, the ribs of beams are exposed. The empty eye sockets of its windows reveal a dim interior of blackened hearth, rotted purlins and straw litter. The warmth has been leached from its walls and the icy wind now carouses at will through its deserted rooms. Like mocking apparitions, a pair of kites appear from nowhere and begin to circle slowly above, eyeing me as if mutely demonstrating their triumph. As the light withers, they slip away as elusively as they appeared.

As I stand there reflecting on the lives the former occupants must have led, a lone male goshawk shears vertically out of the wood and, with an upward stab of its talons, takes a lumbering, unsuspecting magpie from below, then plummets back into the wooded haven with his prey. Only a small puff of feathers, floating on the air is evidence of this swift murder. Although I wait until the light is finally snuffed, hoping to see more of the bird, he remains invisible.

26 DECEMBER

Today I decide to seek the birds of prey at lower altitudes and at the same time burn off some of the excess calories consumed over the Christmas. A long walk along the beach, alongside the crashing waves and the clear air to fill the lungs is the ideal solution.

I start from the small marina on the outskirts of the town, which at this time of year is as quiet as a village chapel at midnight; the metallic slapping of lanyards on aluminium masts above the muffled roar of the sea are the only sounds. I walk on, to the south, beyond the town. Here the coast is untamed. The strong undertow tugs at the pebbly beach, and each pull at the stones produces a thundering roar like a mini-avalanche. The air is abrasive with sea-salt which claws at my exposed skin.

The beach curves away in a wide arc like a scimitar, its blade sparkling in the morning sun. Three over-wintering stonechats flit from fence posts to the ground in search of the few insects around in the short grass. One is a colourful male with crimson breast and snowy cheeks, the others are duller females, speckled brown.

A small group of piping oystercatchers fly in from the sea and land on the beach, their sturdy orange beaks contrasting oddly with their pink legs and their formal pied plumage. Four ringed plovers, invisible until they move, scurry among the seaweed-covered rocks, now exposed by the retreating tide. Just beyond, two cormorants, their bodies hardly discernible above the waterline, dive for flatfish and sand eels. I watch them and time their dives. They remain submerged almost a minute for each dive, sometimes surfacing with a flapping, struggling flounder in their strong mandibles. At the base of the concrete jetty which protects the small harbour, four mouse-like birds are scurrying just above the tide line. Through binoculars, I can discern their scale-like, dark grey-brown backs and yellow legs as they prod diligently into the tiny cracks and crevices for small crustaceans. They are indeed the first purple sandpipers I've seen this year. I'm not sure why, but this concrete harbour wall is always the best place to see them each year. As the tide is pulled back, it sizzles like frying bacon.

In the field which stretches back from the beach to the woods and hills, a small party of five choughs probe for worms alongside crows and jackdaws. From a distance they look no different from their corvid companions, but through binoculars I can discern the tell-tale sheen of their velvet plumage and their finely curved, red-orange beaks and legs which distinguish them clearly from their duller relatives. They are quite trusting, allowing me to approach within 50 metres, before they fly off, to reveal their deeply fissured primaries and emitting their characteristic melodic call note, so different from the throaty expectorations of crows, ravens and rooks or the cackle of jackdaws.

The chough is one of our rarest birds, but is doing very well along the Welsh cliffs and several pairs have established themselves not far from the town. They live on invertebrates they are able to prise from the soil and are thus very susceptible to harsh winters when the ground can become as hard as iron. They find it easier to survive in the milder coastal areas. Attempts by the birds to colonise inland sites have never lasted, probably because the weather there is less clement.

On the grassy banks that rise above the town promenade, surmounted by the castle ruins, seven more choughs are feeding. They are quite unperturbed by the cars and few winter shoppers, allowing me to approach very close, so that I can admire their slender beaks as they probe in the soft soil. On their legs they carry coloured, plastic marker rings. They were probably ringed by the RSPB or BTO to enable a study of their movements to be carried out and monitor their progress. What a morning to see several groups of these rare birds and to have such privileged intimacy!

On the cliff-top, to the north of the town there are at least six dusky rock pipits in residence. These unobtrusive, insectivorous birds also manage to survive the winters by staying in the milder coastal areas and are obviously able to find sufficient sand flies and other suitable food.

The funicular railway, which in Summer takes tourists from the town to the cliff top, is mothballed for the winter. It is a reminder of the Victorian era which gave birth to this small seaside resort. From the summit I look down on the sweep of the bay, bordered by a stately grey terrace of Victorian hotels and, beyond the town, the whole panorama of the bay unfolds. The tall cliffs, which abound with razorbills and guillemots in summer, are only a dull smudge, completing the horizon.

Yet another pair of choughs is probing lower down on the cliff-face, among the tufts of thrift. A male kestrel swings into view and hovers below me, as if suspended on an invisible thread, showing off its flecked, rich chestnut back and slender, dark-tipped wings. A pair of ravens is already nest building below the kestrel on the cliff face. These hardy birds are not perturbed by winter weather and are, with the crossbills, our earliest nesting birds. They sometimes find themselves enveloped by snow storms while sitting on eggs. The young have often left the nests by March or April and the nest site may be taken over by peregrines if there is a shortage of suitable ledges. Even as I watch the ravens carrying thick sticks to build up their nest mound, a pair of peregrines, like two fighter planes, shoot into view and dive bomb the lumbering ravens repeatedly, shrieking angrily, quite clearly afraid of losing their own eyrie to these early interlopers. The heavier female, or falcon, appears suddenly from behind the cliff face and flies upwards as if shot from a catapult. The smaller male, the tiercel, with a few measured, shallow wing beats, follows her. After a few minutes the peregrines disappear over the sea, leaving the ravens to continue their task in peace.

On the rocky shore a small group of oystercatchers are piping animatedly before taking off in a flurry of pied wings over the water, where a pair of cormorants are fishing alongside a red-throated diver, groups of which are regular visitors to this part of the coast in Winter. As I descend the steep cliff-top path, a snipe, not a bird normally associated with cliffs, flies up steeply from the bed of a small stream to drop down in the middle of a caravan site, as if too tired to fly further. It has no doubt been drawn to the coast because it is milder and the ground unfrozen.

Crossbill

I too feel my body has done sufficient penance for my Christmas indulgences and decide to retire to a more hospitable and sheltered place. As I descend to the flatter land, the late afternoon sun sends a few spokes of light through the torn cloud, illuminating the landscape with its pale, dying light. It simulates warmth, but the air remains chilly. The pools and dykes become leaden, but the phragmites reed fringing them is picked out in stark relief together with the trees and small farmsteads, as if embroidered on the cloth of the dark mountains beyond. The low sun throws enormous, etiolated shadows of fence posts and bushes, snaking across the grass.

27 DECEMBER

The hills are now a yellow-ochre colour. I am greeted as I climb up behind the cottage by five ravens croaking in their rough bass as they fly over in a ragged convoy. The upper lakes are exposed to the full blast of the wind. It whiplashes the lake's smooth skin into a puckering of transient scars and welts. A small group of 10 tufted ducks and a single male goosander have sought shelter close to the reed bank, but my arrival forces them out onto the open water. On the second lake a pair of whooper swans, come all the way from their Boreal summer home, has chosen to rest for several days, together with a few pochards and more tufted ducks. The whooper swans are elegant birds with long, straight and slender necks and black and yellow beaks, moving serenely on the water. Their whiteness is dazzling against the dark reeds, as if they are made of Arctic snow. This pair of birds – I presume it to be the same pair – has come to these small, quiet lakes three years running now. On most days in summer the lakes are deserted in terms of bird life, despite the fact that they are well stocked with fish for the local angling club.

The wind is now gathering force and bringing pelting rain, but a short dry spell is utilised by four buzzards to hunt. They hang motionless on the wind, skillfully changing their wing area and angle, letting the wind bear them just a few meters above the ground, their legs dangling, serving as a keel and ready for the pounce. With a small flick of their wings they let the wind rip them backwards like dry leaves. Buzzards are quite sociable birds, unlike goshawks and peregrines, which are very jealous of their nesting territories. They will often, even at the height of the nesting season, circle amicably with other birds quite close to their nests, but in winter this is even more pronounced and you can sometimes see up to five or six birds in the air together. They probably assist each other in locating food, keeping an eye on other circling groups miles away and will soon notice if others have discovered a source of food. On a clear day a buzzard can spot a scurrying rabbit up to two miles away.

It is difficult to remain upright on the hill top. In the plantation the firs are creaking ominously and then ear-splitting cracking sounds presage the crash of one or two huge trees felled like match sticks. Their torn limbs litter the ground in the more exposed parts of the wood. Like the birds, I retreat to my shelter.

By evening the wind is spent. A glorious sunset presents itself with pink and orange tinged, wispy clouds floating on a sky which is a rage of volcanic colour. As the colour drains quickly, a full moon appears over the southern ridge and crystals of frost twinkle in its light on the grass. Dusk is already patrolled by night.

As I enter the front door, I can just make out the soft hooting of a tawny owl not far from the cottage. I hear it twice and then it falls silent, leaving only the crackling and hissing of the logs on the fire to fill the auditory void. I'm reminded of how scarce owls have become. Only the tawny owl seems to be hardy enough to survive countrywide; all our other owls have been badly affected by the destruction of habitats. I have seen one or two visiting short-eared owls around the valley and they turn up regularly on the bog in winter, but long-eared owls are a very scarce breeding bird.

Many years ago, while walking along a field path alongside a tall hawthorn hedge, I saw what looked like a rag flapping on one of the bushes ahead of me. As I came closer I saw it was a little owl which had inadvertently caught its wing on a thorn and was unable to release it. It struggled unsuccessfully and, as I came close, glowered at me through its fearsome, burning eyes - bands of bright chrome surrounding the black coals of the pupils, like rings of fire. I had to run home to grab some gardening gloves before attempting to free it, anxious lest its hook-like talons slashed my bare hands. I placed a BTO ring on its leg and let the bird go. Sadly it was recovered dead only a year later, a few miles from where I'd released it. Birds like this were common in those days, but have now become quite rare sights.

28 DECEMBER

The following morning reveals a landscape rimed so harshly that it looks like snow in the bright, early morning sun. A buzzard flaps leisurely down the valley and into the lower mixed wood. The cold will stay trapped in the valley for several days, but today remains bright and sunny in the short hours between dawn and dusk.

In the field below the cottage magpies are hopping around like huge pied frogs and crows swagger through the stiff grass, searching desperately for food on the frozen ground. On the slope Rusty, the female red kite crouches, looking around forlornly. Its mate, Snowyhead, floats just above and then lands too, in the hope, perhaps, that she has found food. They walk inelegantly together a few short steps over the ice-covered grass, clearly discomforted by the brittle sward. They may be hoping to grab an incautious mole, because, amazingly, the freezing temperatures don't seem to hamper these diligent miners boring in the hillside. Overnight fresh mounds of crumbly, dark soil have been excavated and pushed up into miniature pyramids.

A peregrine, like an anchor flung over the gunwale of the gorse-scabbed ridge, sails over the cottage and is gone in a second. As I cross the lane, I can hear bullfinches wheezing softly in the hedge and I catch the odd flash of rose-pink, soot black or white of a rump in the winter drabness.

A few flurries of snow fall on the hills, but then peter out. The frozen upper lakes now look like sheets of aluminium. Six mallards are stranded on the ice, looking quizzically as if they can't understand why their water is now solid. In a small willow bush, growing among the bulrushes, a pair of buzzards are waiting, eyeing the mallard and hoping for an easy meal, but unsure when to pounce.

A female sparrowhawk swings into an ash tree bordering the lake, also on the lookout for a meal. It dislodges a small party of tits which flies noisily off to another tree. A heron with slow, measured wing beats surveys the lake, in search of some unfrozen water, but continues when it discovers none.

A few miles inland from the cottage is a deep and narrow gorge, its sides densely carpeted with dwarf oaks. A spectacular cataract tumbles over a hundred feet at its narrowest point, carving cauldrons out of the rock at its foot. Above these steep wooded hills, where the gorge broadens out a little, a single kite drifts over.

The house-building couple is still lovingly constructing their replica of an Elizabethan half-timbered cottage with wattle and daub walls. I've watched them over several months as they've erected first the oaken-beam frame, then filled the gaps with mortar and nailed down old slate tiles on the roof. It is already looking like a fixed part of the landscape, with its aged and weathered look. The field surrounding the house, holds two cows and a few sheep and a large flock of mixed fieldfare and redwing are feeding in the grass, the larger, grey-headed fieldfares outnumbering the more slender redwings. I inadvertently snap a twig and the noise ricochets, sending the flock scattering into the surrounding woodland with chattering and rattling expressions of annoyance.

29 DECEMBER

The frost glitters like scattered moondust, but as the sun bleaches the night, it also dissolves the crystals, restoring colour to the landscape.

The bog lies in the valley, flat, like an enormous door mat. It is one of Britain's largest expanses of raised bog and a site of special scientific interest for botanists and naturalists. In winter it attracts peregrinating marsh and hen harriers, as well as groups of kites. There are several kite feeding stations in the area, established by local farmers. What a radical contrast to the persecution these birds suffered in previous decades. It is also a tribute to the tenacity of conservationists that there has been such a dramatic turn-around in public perceptions of the kite.

I can see a dozen kites in the sky over the small, nearby market town and as I watch them drifting past the old granite-stone church tower, I imagine this is how it must have looked

Red Kite

in the Middle Ages, with kites as common as crows and circling over most small towns like this.

During Autumn and Winter when, for the kites, scavenging on the hills can be arduous work, some farmers put out offal for them. Visiting one of these feeding stations to the south of the bog offers me the opportunity of observing numbers of kites at close quarters. I have been invited to this station by Miss Davies, as she introduces herself, proudly emphasising the 'Miss'. She is a tiny, wiry old lady, with a kindly twinkle in her eye. She's been feeding the kites at her farm for several years now. For her they are symbolic for the resilience of the Welsh, their joint ability to survive hardship and persecution. Small sheep farmers like her can identify with the kites; she feels a strong bond with them.

The late afternoon is blustery but dry and she assures me that she will be feeding the kites as usual at four o'clock. She's wearing an old gabardine mac and a large bonnet which completely covers her head, apart from a few wisps of grey hair left protruding. She brings an old fertiliser sack with offal from the barn, slings it over her shoulder and virtually disappears beneath it. She marches down the track - a wobbly plastic sack on spindly legs - towards the field where the kites feed. Already the crows, like old men in funeral garb, sit on the fence posts and in nearby trees, waiting for the offering. A lone kite drifts low over an adjoining field.

As soon as she tips the food out the crows take wing and jostle for the pickings. Within seconds the sky is filled with kites. They seem to appear from nowhere, one after the other, until there are fifteen altogether. They don't land, but allow the crows to pick up the food, then dive-bomb them, forcing them to drop it, so that they can swoop and rob them. This avoids the dangers of landing, when they would become vulnerable.

We watch the birds for some time, being within a hundred meters of the feeding station. I'm fascinated by their aerial skills and the way they shake off the crows' attempts at harassment, like dogs shedding water after a swim. They ride the blustery wind with buoyant ease and total control, their rudder-tails and long wings providing the precision instruments essential for such tight manouevring.

There is an amazing aerial display of birds above the feeding site. I can now count 18 kites in the air at one time, together with half a dozen buzzards and an assortment of crows, ravens and magpies. With each wing beat a kite makes it seems to bounce up with a lightness surprising for such a large bird. The setting sun shimmers on their roan plumage and shines through their translucent feathers, their heads are the colour of dingy snow.

I retire to the farm, where Miss Davies has invited me to tea. It is an old stone farmhouse, opening on to a courtyard, enclosed by outbuildings and barns. The porch and dark doorway is overhung by a thick ivy and I have to duck to enter what seems like a cave. Off the short hallway is the living room, dark stone walls and flagged floor, dominated by a huge, over-roofed hearth. Along two walls are oak dressers adorned with lustre ware, Chinese willow-pattern plates and cups. The mantlepiece is stacked with photos of various relatives, nephews, nieces, uncles and aunts. She bids me sit on one of the cushioned wooden benches, on either side of the hearth, under the chimney hood. She quickly screws up some old newspapers and places them on the flat hearth, piles hazel twigs on top, pours paraffin over it all and lights it with a match. Within minutes we have a roaring fire. To one side of the fire is a large cast-iron door, behind which is the boiler for the hot water. A goose wing lies on the hearth and is used to brush up the ash. Everything is darkened with age and only a dim, golden afternoon light filters in through the one window. I feel as if I am sitting inside a Rembrandt canvas.

She makes the tea and brings a home-baked sponge cake, placing it on a small side table. We drink out of old china cups while she tells me about her sheep farm. She used to teach domestic science in the village school, but didn't like it. She's been running the family farm alone now for a number of years, breeding true Welsh sheep, from an original male she had in 1947. She only feeds the kites in the winter months, knowing that they need to become self-reliant during the breeding season, when there is anyway sufficient 'natural' food available.

During my half-day's excursion over the bog I've seen 49 species of birds, not a bad total for a mid-winter day. As I leave, a thickly-coated fox lopes across one of the frozen fields adjoining the bog. He will be looking for a good hiding place in the reeds from where he can take a fat wigeon or mallard after sunset. It's a good thing for him that he isn't spotted by the group of flat-capped and oilskin clad farmers I passed earlier in the morning, standing beside their Landrovers, egging on the hunt as it caroused through the fields further up the valley.

The ravens and crows, like black rags, flutter to their roosts and I fly back to mine as the dye of night soaks into the watery roseate sky, and frost is already fingering the extremities.

3 JANUARY

The few small birds that remain around the cottage in Winter, mainly tits, are easy to watch in the leafless shrubs and trees. Two pigeons in pearl grey suits, their plump bodies divided from absurdly small heads by their clerical collars, are sitting together like pompous vicars on a branch in the ash tree. Winter thrushes are everywhere feeding in the valley fields and on the berries in the hedgerows. Small flocks of redpolls and siskins are fluttering in the taller birch crowns.

The riparian scene is quiet. The goosanders and mergansers have left for the estuaries and coastal waters and the grey wagtails have moved South. The only bird that appears unperturbed by the seasonal change is the dipper. Where the river flows fast over stony ground it dives repeatedly under the icy flood, undeterred by the temperature.

The river enters the sea softly and gently, flowing into a wide estuary, flanked by glistening banks. It has expended its youthful energies in the mountains that perch on the horizon like breasts above the flat abdomen of the salt flats. It meanders leisurely, slowed by silt and the incoming tide, to mingle with the open sea.

Dipper

First impressions of estuaries are usually disappointing - huge expanses of ugly mud which look devoid of any bird life, but this is an illusion. As soon as I focus my binoculars a new world becomes visible.

The estuary is a gathering place for ducks, waders and gulls, as well as birds of prey. In winter the flocks of waders swirl over it like leaves thrown up in a squall, ducks and geese scar the sky with their dark skeins, shellducks necklace the shoreline.

A red-throated diver flies low over the grey water, passing small groups of see-sawing scoters and a pair of great crested grebes that are pirouetting around each other in early courtship display. On the foreshore three small parties of turnstones are

WINGS OVER THE VALLEY

flicking the pebbles in search of small crustacea. Two redshanks join them there. The sun's cold light turns the receding tide into a diamond-encrusted shawl wrapped around the bay.

This part of the coast boasts the largest phragmites reedbed in mid-Wales and it stretches before me to the horizon. It's a spot where I always expect surprises - birds like spoonbill, bittern and shrike have been seen here occasionaly - but I rarely catch a glimpse of such rarities. Three over-wintering stonechats sit stoically on frost-rimed hogweed umbels and a pair of reed buntings is bustling close by in the reeds. The early morning sun has turned the reeds into a rippling of silver blades. As I slowly scan its undulating surface, a buzzard-like bird enters my field of view. Could it be perhaps...? As it flies leisurely just above the waving seed brushes its wings form a shallow 'V' and it glides for a few seconds before flapping again. It is indeed a marsh harrier! A male with pale grey wing patches. This bird remains into the early spring and there is always the hope that such a male may find a mate and breed someday. One or two marsh harriers are regular winter visitors here. I spend the day wandering around the edge of the bog and among the nearby coastal dunes but see nothing more unexpected. Only as the tide retreats do the waders and wigeon gather again.

A duck shooter wanders out along the dyke, silhouetted against the dusk sky, his grey gun hanging loosely over his shoulder like an innocent golf club. The mangled carcass of a dead mallard lying on the dyke wall is evidence of his bloody sport. In the far distance waders wheel and turn in perfect synchronised motion and as their undersides catch the evening light they look like swirls of snowflakes. Oystercatchers fly up from the tideline, as the flood advances, to realight further up river.

Male hen harrier

As it darkens and the lights in the town flicker into life, clouds of starlings, like bees around a hive, swarm from inland to roost on the pier in their thousands.

13 JANUARY

This year's exceptionally mild winter has thrown nature out of gear. Although the growth and reproductive cycles of both animals and plants are governed largely by the length of day, temperature is quite obviously also important. The relatively warm, moist weather has brought out swarms of midges, awakened slumbering house flies and a variety of butterflies. Daffodil and bluebell spears protrude above the soil and the buds on some hawthorn and elderberry bushes have already broken into leaf. Resident birds are actively establishing nesting territories and are in full song. A pair of house sparrows is already nest building in one of the bird boxes.

I only hope there is not a sudden drop of the barometer, which would have serious repercussions on this delicate yearly cycle. The signs are not good: An angry sky is boiling over the hills and fitful gusts are rocking the trees.

The surface of the upper lakes is puckered. The old sluice gate rises from the water like a gaunt scaffold, its beams eroded and lichen-encrusted. Four 'red-heads' (female mergansers) launch from the water as I approach and fly low inland, following the stream's sinuous route, to seek a less disturbed water. A reed bunting calls sleepily from the tangle of dead grass and reed at the lakeside. Tatters of dark keys hang from an ash tree, silhouetted against the backdrop of a tarnished silver sky. I hurry down the hillside as the sun vacates its celestial post for a sharp moon, which casts its pallor into the cold, steely night.

11 FEBRUARY

I only manage to leave the cottage by mid-morning, so decide on a short trip to the estuary and stretch of coast to the north. I have been told that an over-wintering great grey shrike can still be seen around the willow scrub on the adjoining bog and I also hope to see a few other lingering winter migrants.

The day is crisp, bright and mild for the time of year. The

estuary glitters in the light, but there is hardly a bird to be seen. A couple from a dog sanctuary have brought a van-load of dogs with them and are walking them at the water's edge, not exactly increasing my prospects of seeing much! Two pairs of redshanks have found some tranquility on the river bank, a few mallards are far out on the salt marsh, together with some curlews, but there is no sign of wigeon. pintail or of winter waders.

The bog, too, is in fact as lifeless today as it appears. There is no sign of the shrike or anything else. There are no harriers or hunting peregrine and, as yet, no summer migrants. Only a few itchy meadow pipits starting up from the dyke banks. I am about to depart when out of the corner of my eye I catch a pale flutter of wings against the willow carr, but it disappears again before I can recognise it. I think it is probably a gull, but something is not quite right and my curiosity nudges me to investigate. I creep towards where it has vanished. The apparition suddenly reappears and glides into view on silent, rounded wings, its moon-like face intently scrutinising the ground. Although it is midday and the sun is shining, this barn owl is out hunting. The light exaggerates its ghostly persona, lending its creamy-yellow plumage an ethereal aura as the bird floats in front of the tenebrous curtain of willow. It ignores my close presence and lands on a fence post, rotating its bulbous head, watching for any movement and listening for rustling sounds in the swathes of dessicated grass and sedge. Then it takes off again, flapping rhythmically, quartering the bank, its huge eyes, like dark chestnuts on the saucer of its face mask. Its overly large head gives it a top-heavy appearance, as if it has no body, just legs and wings. I am able to watch it for half an hour before it eventually retreats into the willow thicket.

My disappointment at missing the rare shrike and seeing little else, is amply compensated by this elegant performance in broad daylight.

21 FEBRUARY

An ineffectual sun is contending with the mist and rain. The day is blustery with alternating showers and bright spells. From the overhung lane, I look up at a sky cobwebbed by bare twigs. The woods in the distance are lent a dark purple sheen by the filigree of unopened birch and alder catkins. The hazel's catkins, though, are already open, yellow-dusting the hedgerows and woodland fringes.

Kites, like most resident birds, establish their territories very early in the year. I'm on tenterhooks to find out whether Snowyhead and Rusty will again breed in the valley this year, or whether the farmer's bracken-clearing on the southern hillside or the plantation tree-felling have caused enough disturbance to dissuade them; they are, after all, birds of the quiet, secluded valleys.

I remain up on the hill and can lie on the ground, which is dry, and actually sunbathe as the sun is surprisingly hot for this time of the year. After several hours, I spot a large bird of prey flapping slowly but purposefully up the valley towards me. Through binoculars I can see it's Snowyhead, the male kite, alone and carrying a thick stick in its talons. I remain absolutely still and track his movements. He is keeping low to the ground, whether because the stick is heavy and cumbersome or whether to remain unobtrusive, I don't know. He then rises over the lake to glide down towards the beech copse and lands in one of the large trees. Because they are still bare, I'm able to watch him arranging the stick in a fork near the top. Satisfied with its positioning, he flies off and I don't catch even a glimpse of him again before dusk, like a smoky haze, begins to bleed through the trees. I'm thrilled. This is a sure sign that they've decided to settle here. I hope fervently that they will remain undisturbed from hominid activities during the next critical weeks, and that will include me too!

22 FEBRUARY

The night brings heavy rainfall, but it has ceased by morning, the clouds have dispersed and the sun is again challenging the season. The valley streams are gushing with water. White threads are unspooling down the mountain-sides. Although there are few birds about, walking in the winter sunshine is a keen pleasure. Kites and buzzards are making full use of the weather to circle over their territories, buoyant on the rising warm air. The moor is now becoming itchy like a rough-woven shirt on the bare back of the hill. As I walk, pipits spring like champagne corks from its matted weave.

In a fold of the valley is a small oakwood and I traverse it on my way down. As I patter through the mouldering leaves, the rusty brown ghost of a woodcock rises from the deep litter, a metre or so in front of me and, after a short flight on whispering wings, drops into a thicket of young larches. The wet, but mild winter has brought good numbers of them into the area, where they can more easily probe deep into the moist and soft earth for food.

A monastic silence is imposed on the wood and I encounter nothing else until I reach the river. It is in full flood, its waters surging, twisting and tonguing around the rocks, as it snakes towards the sea. As I emerge from the wood, a loud chattering interspersed with whistling notes separates out from the background slurping and sucking of the water. On a large stone in mid-stream a pristine pair of dippers are displaying. They face each other and indulge in intensive wing-shivering, head stretching and 'bobbing'. Dippers undertake such pair-bonding very early in the year and are not disconcerted by cold temperatures. Their plumage is thicker than any other passerine and is kept waterproof by oil from their large oil gland. It is not really known why dippers 'bob' or wagtails 'tail-wag', but it may have something to do with stimulating the oil glands which ensures their plumage stays dry. Dippers' wings are stubby and strong, enabling them to swim underwater, a little like penguins.

This fast-flowing, wide stretch of river is ideal for them. It is quite shallow, flowing over a pebbly bed and there are long stretches of steep, overgrown banks which offer perfect concealment for their nest. Dippers prefer streams and rivers rich in calcereous salts, where crustaceans and insect larvae flourish and are therefore commoner to the East, but although the rivers nearer the coast are more acidic, I can always encounter a pair every mile or so. Its Welsh names, 'Trochwr', the plunger or the more poetic one: 'Bronwen y Garw', whitebreast of the torrent, are wonderfully descriptive of one of our most intriguing water birds.

There is a stiff wind on the coast, but in the troughs of the waves there are small rafts of ten or twelve scoter no more than a few hundred metres offshore.

In the distance, over the estuary, two brown merlins are hunting. I can't make out whether they are adult females or juveniles. They are dashing low over the ground and I lose them as they swerve below the horizon and their colour melts into that of the mud flats. About 50 shelduck are strung out along the river bank, feeding with small parties of curlews and redshank.

The sky hangs like an enormous curtain around the flat stage, heightening the expectancy of some great theatrical performance. Then as if to justify my choice of simile, shafts of sunlight suddenly stab through the clouds, to spotlight a patch of reeds, place a halo around a group of distant trees and, with facile alchemy, transmute the leaden dyke water into rippling silver. However no drama unfolds, only the distant flickering of unidentifiable waders and ducks at the far edge, as they startle up and then settle again.

A male kestrel hovers over a field at the roadside, his ash-grey head bent as he focuses on the ground. He drops as if the thread suspending him has suddenly snapped. He's caught a vole and rises with it clutched in his yellow talons. At that very moment one of the merlins reappears right behind the kestrel and also pounces on the ground, then flies off, taking its prey to be devoured in a more secluded spot, away from my prying eyes.

The late afternoon is clear and bright. On my way home, I see within one hour, two parties of eight and six buzzards in the air together and then a raven competing with three kites over a sheep carcass. The kites are, I believe, young birds, as their upper parts are a pale creamy buff and the copper feathers of their tails are bright and fresh. On one of the pools in the upper valley village, two coots, like washed up clumps of coal, are asleep at the water's edge. They are by no means permanent residents here and I'm always pleased to see them.

23 FEBRUARY

A wild storm rages all night and I sleep fitfully. The roof beams groan and the branches of the ash flail about, threatening to detach themselves. The rain whip-lashes the windows. The trees shudder under the downpour. I am not looking forward to the day, but as morning breaks, I am seduced from my bed by sun streaming into the room and pools of blue floating past the panes. The wind is still tormenting the trees, but the rain has ceased. A blue-glazed sky holds a throbbing sun and the grass shimmers like a sheet of water under its caress. The local buzzard pair brings me fully awake with insistent mewing as they twirl over their domain.

Snowyhead appears above the mountain behind the cottage, flying into the wind with laboured wing beats. It buffets him upwards, until he becomes the size of a skylark. He hangs there for a minute or two, then, as if surrendering to the stronger force, is swept inland.

The roof of the bird box on the terrace has been wrenched off in the night by the wind, so I fix it more securely. In the shelter of the honeysuckle on the wall, a blackbird huddles. A small party of chattering crossbills is catapulted towards the firs in the lower valley. Other birds have been driven to ground.

26 FEBRUARY

The wind is still forceful, driving high cumulus cloud in flocks across the hills. The sun shoots shafts of warm light through the gaps and I imagine I can feel the first tentative pangs of spring's labour.

The nearby 'Scottish Glen' is sheltered by its steep mountainsides, cradling the slender thread of silver river that traverses its length. Its woods are still quiet, awaiting the onrush of the spring invasion. Even so, I'm surprised at the range of bird life I am able to see on my four hour walk - 25 different species. Coal tits and goldcrests gambol capriciously in the crowns of the firs, a pair or two of siskins seep as they fly over, pied wagtails tremble at the river's edge and there is a large mixed flock of chaffinches and bramblings feeding beneath a stand of oaks in a small field. Several of the bramblings are already decked in their peach and glossy, pinot-noir summer plumage and must be about to depart eastwards for their breeding territories.

A peregrine flies unhurriedly up the valley, as if looking for suitable nesting cliffs, and a male goshawk circles over a likely nesting site, its barred wings and tail fanned to catch the full uplift of the weak thermal.

A single curlew calls plaintively from a marshy meadow and I wonder if it too intends nesting because I haven't heard or seen one there in previous years.

As I tread with muted steps over the springy grass track through a young larch plantation, a fox crosses my path a few meters ahead and only when he looks by chance in my direction, does he then break into a lope, his chestnut coat and luxurious brush glistening in the glancing morning light. He is no doubt on the prowl for resting hares or a careless pheasant among the young trees.

28 MARCH

The peregrines should be returning to their eyries by now, so I decide to visit one of the wilder sites, which is also, because of its relative inaccessibility, one of the safest.

It's a short walk along a narrow forestry track, then a clamber over rough moorland with a detour around a dark, quiescent lake which bleeds into the narrow gorge. After leaving the forestry track, the enigmatic wildness of the moor captivates and simultaneously unsettles me. It is forbidding and soundless, not another being to be heard or seen, simply the boundless expanse under an interminable sky.

I scramble over rocks, down a dank gully into the narrow gorge where I'm confronted by a sheer wall of rock that towers to the sky. I feel trapped and menaced in this natural fortress dungeon. No one knows I'm here and if I fall and need help, no one would hear my cries. The realisation of my lonesomeness and insignificance is awesome. My contemplation is suddenly shattered by a hectoring screaming from above. I can't see the bird on the dark face even when I scan it with binoculars. Its screams reverberate around the gorge, having no clear point of origin. Only when I clap my hands, does she - for it is indeed the heavier falcon - swoop from a ledge and reveal her whereabouts.

The twigs are still rimed with hoar frost. But hawthorn hedges in the more sheltered valleys are already revealing pin-heads of green as their buds cautiously begin to break. Then, a new sound invades my aural space, a voice awaited impatiently over the long dull days: a fragile piccolo tsilp-tsalp from the upper, sun warmed extremities of the big ash tree by the house. The chiff chaff, one of our first returning migrants has arrived back in the valley, heralding the return of spring. It is like hearing the strains of a beloved melody after many years, and I can't help smiling contentedly to myself.

CHECKLIST OF BIRDS SEEN IN AND AROUND THE VALLEY

Magpie pair

C H E C K L I S T   O F   B I R D S   S E E N   I N   A N D   A R O U N D   T H E   V A L L E Y

Grey Heron

Spoonbill

Little Egret

Whooper Swan

Mute Swan

Canada Goose

Barnacle Goos

White-fronted Goose

Grey-lag Goose

Mallard

Pintail

Wigeon

Shoveler

Teal

Garganey

Goldeneye

Scaup

Tufted Duck

Pochard

Common Scoter

Eider

Merganser

Goosander

Shelduck

Water Rail

Moorhen

Coot

Common Buzzard

Sparrowhawk

Goshawk

Marsh Harrier

Hen Harrier

Red Kite

Osprey

Peregrine Falcon

Merlin

Kestrel

Wood Pigeon

Rock Dove

Stock Dove

Collared Dove

Snipe

Woodcock

Greenshank

Redshank

Green Sandpiper

Purple Sandpiper

Common Sandpiper

Dunlin

Turnstone

Knot

Sanderling

Oystercatcher

Curlew

Whimbrel

Black-tailed Godwit

Bar-tailed Godwit

Grey Plover

Golden Plover

Ringed Plover

Little Ringed Plover

Lapwing

Dotterel

Guillemot

Razorbill

Great Skua

Great Black-backed Gull

Lesser Black-backed Gull

Common Gull

Herring Gull

Mediterranean Gull

Herring Gull

Black-headed Gull

Kittiwake

Fulmar

Sandwich Tern

Common Tern

Red Grouse

Black Grouse

Pheasant

Quail

Spotted Crake

Barn Owl

Tawny Owl

Short-eared Owl

Long-eared Owl

Cuckoo

Nightjar

Great Spotted Woodpecker

Lesser-spotted Woodpecker

Green Woodpecker

Skylark

Swift

Sand Martin

House Martin

Swallow

Magpie

Jay

Carrion Crow

Jackdaw

Rook

Raven

Chough

Starling

Goldcrest

Dipper

Tree Creeper

Nuthatch

Wren

Blue Tit

Great Tit

Coal Tit

Marsh Tit

Willow Tit

Long-tailed Tit

Blackbird

Song Thrush

Mistle Thrush

Fieldfare

Redwing

Ring Ouzel

Wheatear

Whinchat

Stonechat	Dunnock
Robin	
Redstart	
Reed Warbler	
Cetti's Warbler	
Grasshopper Warbler	
Sedge Warbler	
Blackcap	
Common Whitethroat	
Lesser Whitethroat	
Willow Warbler	
Chiffchaff	
Wood Warbler	
Meadow Pipit	
Rock Pipit	
Grey Wagtail	
Pied Wagtail	
Spotted Flycatcher	
Pied Flycatcher	
Great Grey Shrike	
Bullfinch	
Linnet	
Redpoll	
Crossbill	
Chaffinch	
Greenfinch	
Siskin	
Goldfinch	
Brambling	
Yellow Hammer	
Reed Bunting	
House Sparrow	
Tree Sparrow	